LOOKING FROM BEHIND YOUR EYES

Your Mind Is Your Business.
Learn How To Direct It.

EVAN WORLDWIND

Copyright © 2023 Evan Worldwind.

All rights reserved. This book is protected by copyright. No part of this book may be reproduced or transmitted in any form or by any means, including as photocopies or scanned-in or other electronic copies, or utilized by any information storage and retrieval system without written permission from the copyright owner.

ISBN: 979-8-9886440-0-2

Interior design by FormattedBooks

I dedicate this book to my beloved Rosa,
my children, Makeda and Goddard, as well as my
families in the United States and Barcelona.

CONTENTS

Acknowledgments vii
About Looking from behind Your Eyes ix
Preface xi
The Dreamer Inside xiii

PART 1

Introduction 3
Introducing Exercise Guide 5
4-Minute Stance 7
36-Day Challenge 9
Reason for the 36-Day Challenge 11
Sequencing Set 13
This Section of Practices 15
Dreams and Stories 17
The Symbolic Nature of Numbers 19
What is the 13 Joints Exercise? 23
Minding Your Business 25
Experience is Better than Explaining 29
Section 1: The 36-Day Challenge 31
Section 2: Sequencing Set 61
Section 3: Meditation at Bedtime 77
Looking without Judgment 83
Honoring the Body 85
Retirement is a Waste 87
Habits Are Not Permanent 89
Your First Thought is a Gut Feeling 91
Rushing for the Deadman Road 93

PART 2

The Artist's Dream Principles & Ideas 99
Preparing to Write...103
Dead Man's Face in the Mirror 105
Your Life is Your Right to Live..109
The Story of Duppies...113
Self-Sabotaging 119
Nowhere to Look but Inside..121
Satisfaction in Sharing 125
Believing is Taking Action 127
Rider in the Dream.. 129
Having Command of the Mind 133
Integrity is a Valuable Principle 137
I Can Forgive, but I will Never Forget...........................139
Journey of Self-Discovery 141
Claim Ownership of Your Power....................................143
Mr. & Mrs. Lover Lovers 147
Mother's Teachings 151
Clearing for New Explorations.. 155
Keep Your Hands Up 157
Psychic Self-Imprisonment 161
Amplification of Thoughts..163
The Challenge of Empowerment.....................................167
Looking for a Plan to Take Action 169
Implement the Principles...171

Conclusion...173
About the Author..177
Appreciation...179
About the Book Cover Illustration 181
Bibliography...183

ACKNOWLEDGMENTS

I wish to express my gratitude to my beloved Rosa for her love and support. I am extremely thankful to Maricarme Riera Prunera, my writing coach and book designer.

A special thanks to Ben Gerstein for his contributions to the first proof and book outline.

To my father, Daniel, and mother, Josephine; I want to convey my heartfelt appreciation and forever love for their unwavering inspiration.

To my board of directors, much love and gratitude.

ABOUT LOOKING FROM BEHIND YOUR EYES

"What I Hear I Forget, What I See I
Remember, What I Do I Understand."
—Chinese Proverb

Looking From Behind Your Eyes is an action-taking manuscript, a personal transmission to help you to design definite plans for taking ownership of your creative power. This book provides you with clear, effective internal-focus exercises, inspiring stories, visionary dreams of taking command of your business: your mind. Also included are bedtime meditations for your night school training.

In addition, there is a 36-Day Challenge to jump-start your new world—a structured grid to help you to claim your gift—the gift of being present with your visions and goals. Your artist's dream doorway, leading you into a state of magnificence where you learn to stand alone without feeling lonely. That sacred place where you live, objectifying your truth with courage and strength.

Looking From Behind Your Eyes challenges you to do the great work bubbling inside of you. It is your sacred manifesto, whispering in your head to be impeccable to the highest degree. An indisputable being with a purpose in mind, instead of your world's best-kept secret. Here is an encouraging thought for you: Answer your "why"!

Why Am I Doing What I Am doing? Who Am I? This book implores you, the seeker of significant experiences, to open up. Yes! You are feeling it inside to re-envision your past and shift your attention to your present state, where your visions and goals live.

Read it now! Dedicated to the artist dreamer in you.

Richest blessings,
www.evanworldwind.com

PREFACE

Do Something Now

Every time I reflect on my identity and purpose, I hear this inner voice say, "Stop thinking so much and do something." Whatever you want. I simply remind myself how easy it can be to Do Something.

In one of my cherished memories of "Doing Something," I lay on my back in a grassy area beneath my father's bamboo orchard, gazing at the sky through the branches and relishing the moment. Thunder echoed through my head as the branches clashed together. Watching the sun's rays peek through the branches was nothing less than a heavenly encounter. This childhood experience is the guiding light in my life's work.

My wish is for you to experience heaven in the present moment. Listen to your music, the song that only you can sing, and affirm that you are a spirit being, an artist showcasing your greatness whose destiny guides you, and whose stories support you. I am my friend who constantly motivates me to push past my fears and pursue my creative endeavors. I am the editor of my story, the adviser of my thoughts, and the path I choose for my present future is my responsibility.

Get it done. Do something that brings you joy.

THE DREAMER INSIDE

Why I Wrote This Book

This book is a collection of fragments of my life to create a coherent narrative that explains the significance of my experiences.

There are primary reasons why I wrote this book. First, my soul's mission is to collect information, gain experiences, and share all of it with people who are just different aspects of myself. I had a strong desire to live a fulfilling life for a long time. It is a feeling where I stand alone but don't feel lonely, and stand my ground regardless of what happens. I wrote this book for people whose internal chatter resonates with my "why."

Second, I accepted that my conscience was directing me to write this book. I envisioned a mother who had just completed a nine-month journey of emotional, psychological, and physical experiences, now beginning a new journey of caring and guiding her baby. I felt like this newborn who relied entirely on the love and care of its mother to survive.

Finally, my words about the subjective world are for those passionate individuals who want to speak the truth that resonates with their heart. This is for those who have realized that searching outside themselves for answers is a waste of time. For the curious individuals seeking answers to their questions about who they are and in what direction they should focus their attention.

If you're looking to take control of your own wellness, this book is for you. I meant this for individuals who desire to step up and give their imagination the recognition it deserves.

This presentation bears resemblance to tai chi, if you are familiar with it. The physical and mental exercises in this book are easy on your body and will blow your mind if you do them daily. So, brace yourself!

This psychological journey reveals the hidden potential inside you that yearns for expression, despite the sacrifices. Your awareness as a director will no longer be inactive. You're greater than your personality, labels, and stories.

PART 1

INTRODUCTION

It's Never Too Late to Start a Routine

You can revolutionize your life through a twenty-minute daily exercise routine. I will answer your questions regarding your body, mind, and the practical, down-to-earth purpose of your life.

You can take care of yourself even with a busy lifestyle. Waiting for change or procrastinating on creating a better life for yourself will only lead to negative feelings and a lurking sense of unease.

People who struggle with anxiety and depression have found remarkable success in implementing the basic mental and physical tools that are provided here. Emotional drama, such as blaming others or self-judgment, didn't define your entry into this world. Your purpose is to ignite the bravery to recall your true essence. Look toward the horizon with your radiant eyes.

Sharing an empowered version of yourself with your friends and family is the ultimate gift you can give. Don't procrastinate on manifesting the beauty of your mind.

While assisting others in conquering their limiting beliefs, I am aware of communicating with two parts of them: their objective physical self, and their subjective mental states. The physical self requires a sense of security to transmit sensory data, while the subjective mental healer within needs a mindful inner space for optimal outcomes. In this conversation that starts in silence, I will disclose effective ways to take charge of your life.

There is no available book with a magical solution to fulfill your desires. The solution to your needs already exists within you, and it drives your experiences. As a result, these experiences hold significant value. Use them as a roadmap to manifest your current aspirations and shape your reality.

I wrote this book in two parts. Part 1 involves a conversation with you, along with detailed guidance on using internal-focus exercises.

Our intimate communication is built upon the foundation of the 4-Minute Stance exercise, which can be found in these pages. You'll face a 36-day program ahead that encompasses a variety of internal exercises. The 36-Day Challenge consists of exercises such as the 13 Joints Exercise, Eyes Orbiting the Sun, Scapular Muscle Engagement, and Reverse Meditation, which help you prepare for night schooling.

Part 2 contains inspiring stories and visionary dreams that will motivate you to continue with the exercises. My goal is to present you, the reader, with my personal stories and dreams to inspire you to direct your highest vision with no apologies. I hope you unleash your potential and fly high.

Internal art has been my focus for over twenty years, with the foundation laid by the 36-Day Challenge and other exercises. I provide a straightforward format for you to use, regardless of where you are in your life journey.

I urge you to recognize your worth and claim it.

INTRODUCING EXERCISE GUIDE

Part 1 appears in a specific order:

1. 4-Minute Stance
2. 36-Day Challenge
3. Sequencing Set

4-MINUTE STANCE

All the physical exercises in this book are built on the foundation of the 4-Minute Stance. This is where the 36-Day Challenge and Sequencing Set start. It's important to practice the 4-Minute Stance before moving on to other physical exercises.

36-DAY CHALLENGE

- 13 Joints Exercise
- Scapular Muscle Engagement
- Pressing Between Walls
- Eyes Orbiting

The 36-Day Challenge is an effective method for integrating physical and mental exercise forms into your body matrix. It takes thirty-six days for a shift to occur in your physiology. It is a time-consuming process to merge the mind and body to cultivate new roots.

After finishing the 13 Joints Exercise, you will need to do three more exercises: Scapular Muscle Engagement, Pressing Between Walls, and Eyes Orbiting. Consider them as a summary of the 36-Day Challenge.

The Scapular Muscle Engagement and Pressing Between Walls exercises are essential for relieving muscle tension in the body. Perform these two exercises consecutively after your regular physical exercise routine.

The Eyes Orbiting exercise is great for relaxing your facial area and focusing your attention on the rotation of your eyes. This exercise will help you connect with your environment without grabbing on to external images.

It is important to practice each step in the 36-Day Challenge in order, as they form a compound foundation for part 2. Use the 4-Minute Stance as your starting point for each practice to avoid knee discomfort.

REASON FOR THE 36-DAY CHALLENGE

The 36-Day Challenge will help you feel your body in cohesion with your internal self expression. From my experience, the 13 Joints Exercise appears simple, yet it will challenge your mind to stay focused on the detailed description of each exercise.

36-Day Calendar

First, read and get the basic understanding of the 13 Joints Exercise. Then establish a specific date to start your journey. Mark off the thirty-six days on your calendar, starting with day one. On day thirty-six, write: "I completed my 36-Day Challenge."

If you miss a day in your practice, start over from day one until you can go the full thirty-six days without missing a day. This is to make sure you give yourself a chance to internalize these circular energy movements. Once you complete the 36-Day Challenge and have a good grasp of the exercise steps, you can then move on to part 2.

A Warning Here

There is no self-judgment in your practice. Love yourself no matter what challenges you may face. Learn to transform any self-doubts or negative thoughts into positive thoughts and images that are empowering and resonate with your work. Later, in part 2 of the book, I'll introduce you to a transforming meditation. It will aid you in revising your thoughts.

Keep this journey to yourself and do your loving best to stick with it. This is You, Your Life, Your Design. After each practice, take a few minutes to record how you feel. Whatever stories come to your mind, take time to write them down. Taking the time to contemplate your thoughts that pertain to your practice will aid you tremendously with your energy cultivation.

SEQUENCING SET

- Four Corners, Four Wheels
- Figure Eight
- Sitting Observation Technique

By using the Sequencing Set, you learn to move your body as a cohesive unit, synchronizing the movements of your hips, shoulders, and hands. Although it may seem challenging, it is possible to master it if you dedicate time to focus your attention daily.

The purpose of the Four Corners Exercise is to teach you how to focus on the sockets of your shoulders and hips, which are energized by the spiraling of your spinal column.

The Figure Eight exercise involves rotating your hips and shoulders together while focusing on the center of the sacrum. The movement of your hips and shoulders together results in a figure-eight-like motion of your hands, where two circles converge at the edge.

The Sitting Observation Technique can help calm your nervous system, particularly after exercising or a busy workday.

THIS SECTION OF PRACTICES

- Reverse Meditation
- Diaphragm Observation
- The Observer Technique

This section prepares you to unite with the subconscious, creative aspect of yourself. It is imperative that you complete your day with a positive feeling, because your subconscious receives whatever your state of mind impresses upon it. Prepare your body and mind as if you are getting ready to step into your love chamber to meet your lover. Your state of mind determines your experience in night school, with your subconscious energy in motion.

Reverse Meditation involves reviewing your daily activities in reverse, allowing you to correct any undesirable events retroactively.

Diaphragm observation involves allowing the rhythm of your breath to be expressed in your body without exerting too much effort.

The Observer Technique exercise suggests listening to the silent voice inside as you visualize the expansion of your breathing.

DREAMS AND STORIES

In part 2, I share my dreams and stories to establish a heart-to-heart connection with you, urging you to take ownership of the gems of your experiences.

Your attention and willingness to engage with me in the never-ending story of self-discovery is truly appreciated.

DREAMS AND STORIES

THE SYMBOLIC NATURE OF NUMBERS

Before I proceed any further, let me provide you with an example of how important the numbers (36, 9, 4, 12) and the enigmatic number 13 can be. My perspective on these numbers may assist you with creating your own interpretation of them. If you are interested, here are the links to explore the world of numerology.

The numerological sum of 36 is 9 when you add 3 and 6, and multiplying 9 by 4 gives you 36. The number 36 represents the 36-Day Challenge. The 9 signifies the human journey before birth, while the 4 represents the four corners observed in the exercise sets found in this book.

Inner awareness of the body and mind is key when working with the provided exercises. "The essence of numerology number 36 represents energies that accomplish creative goals for helping humankind. Above all else, 36 is a humanitarian. It won't always come up with creative solutions to what it identifies as problems. But it's always concerned about the welfare of humanity."[1]

---

[1] Will Bontrager, "Number 36 Meaning," Affinity Numerology, Will Bontrager Software LLC, accessed September 19, 2023, https://affinitynumerology.com/number-meanings/number-36-meaning.php.

"The deep-down basic essence of numerology, number 9 is a concern for the welfare of humanity. It is a creative, tolerant, and compassionate existence generous with its help for individuals and organizations intent on doing the world some good."[2]

The number 12 has widespread usage in religious texts, zodiac cycles, and months of the year, but Ethiopians use a thirteen-month calendar.

Countless information exists about the number 12, which can be divided by the sum of 1+2=3. The number also represents the twelve tones of the Western chromatic musical scale. We are the ultimate body, mind, and spirit instrument. These twelve tones comprise the seven natural intervals, with five sharp/flat intervals in between the natural tones.

The unknown meaning of a story is what we fear.

The story of the number 13 is undefined but believed to be unlucky and that it should be avoided. Why is that? It is a mystery to everyone. We accept the warning without question. The mind ventures to comprehend the generally accepted theory by creating stories that attach to our unfortunate experiences that shape our perception.

"Many people can feel fear of the number 13 and its vibrations, but this is actually one of the hardest things or misunderstandings of its meaning in a numerology chart. When you understand the true power of this number, you see that there is nothing to be afraid of. The number 13

---

[2] Bontrager, "Number 9 Meaning."

presents itself in a birthday number, your numerology number, or in compound numbers!"[3]

Most information is understandable when shared with a good intention in a simple format. To illustrate, I am using the number 13 to emphasize the thirteen joints linking the human anatomy, then summing up 1+3 to get 4. The 4 now represents the four corners of our torso. You will learn the importance of these numbers in the exercises given in sections 1 and 2. These aspects of the moving exercises require your full attention.

"Think of four walls in a room or four legs on a chair," Wolfe says. "(Four) is the number of support and stability, so it is about rooting down and taking care of your life."[4] I will explain further in the Four Corners Exercise.

The crucial aspect of the numbers in this book is how they relate to the exercise forms and repetitions, creating a motivating flow in your practice. If we take a moment to appreciate our surroundings, we can see that the flow is all around us.

Have fun playing with these numbers. As you practice, they will help you to truly connect with your temple body in geometric and psychological ways.

---

[3] Sarah Scoop, "The Meaning and Symbolism of the Angel Number 13 in Numerology," *Sarah Scoop*, accessed September 19, 2023, https://sarahscoop.com/the-meaning-and-symbolism-of-the-angel-number-13-in-numerology.

[4] Natalie Arroyo Camacho and Rebecca Norris, "The Angel Number 4 is Basically Your Ancestors Giving You a Support Hug," *Well and Good*, last modified August 25, 2023, https://www.wellandgood.com/angel-number-4.

WHAT IS THE 13 JOINTS EXERCISE?

This exercise form focuses primarily on the thirteen major joints connecting the entire structure of the physical body.

The thirteen major joints are the ankles, knees, hips, shoulders, elbows, wrists, and neck. They are the spinning, energetic junctions of the body. Think of them as the thirteen departments forming your business, your cooperation that is managed by you, the Chief Executive Officer. As the CEO, you direct each of the thirteen departments with your mind resource.

By consciously engaging in improving your body's physiology with the 13 Joints Exercise, you can take ownership of your mind. First we start with the individual joints, and then coordinate them as one movement.

After the 36-day journey, the rejuvenation and positive feelings you have given yourself will amaze you. This is your business of self-reliance. Keep building on it how you see fit.

After each practice, take a few minutes to record how you feel. Whatever stories come to your mind, take time to write them down. Taking this time to contemplate your thoughts that pertain to your practice will aid you tremendously in your personal development.

Before we begin, let us discuss what it means to mind your business.

MINDING YOUR BUSINESS

How many times have you heard someone say "Mind your business" as a way to tell someone else to be quiet? The statement is telling you to take care of your own affairs. Ponder on it, with no criticism. It is likely that the initial step in taking care of your own affairs is to have some quiet time to think, wouldn't you say? Metaphysical writings suggest that effective time management involves focusing on the mind first to promote healing, or achieve goals.

Just like a gardener, the initial step to minding your business involves preparing the soil before planting the seeds. Once the gardener has planted the seeds, the only remaining chore is to maintain the external environment of the garden. An internal source manages all subterranean tasks. This entire process is being handled from two different perspectives: the external work of the gardener, and the internal source: the architect of the subjective world.

View yourself as two distinct entities: the gardener and the internal architect, who coexist in one physical form. The gardener represents your external senses, while the internal architect represents your internal creative thoughts. Your internal thoughts are personal imaginings that fuel your desire to build or expand something. External nature reflects your human personality and the idea of self, shaping your reality.

Your physical being is also a temple, a sacred chariot for spiritual oneness, the source of all, a spiritual entity with a deep imagination, a marvelous component of the human experience. I define the physical body as an elongated temple—a tabernacle of energy that warps in radiant, breathable skin and experiences its creative realities.

The Gardener and the Architect

Here is a conversation with my two selves (the Gardener and the Architect) about minding my own business:

Gardener: Why do I waste so much time thinking about what I would like to do, but afraid to take action?

Architect: You are asking instead of accepting? When you say you want something, your tires are reeling in the mud of your fear, but you're not moving forward. Your desire for a thing is already alive in your imagination.

Gardener: Your answer makes little sense to me.

Architect: Here is a verse from the Bible that has made little sense to most people for generations: "The Lord is my Shepherd; I shall not want."[5] You say that you want something, your senses are affirming you do not have it. You are living in a world ruled by the senses, justifying your awakened state as a reality. This reality hardens with limiting ideas—your ideas of self that control you and rob you of your gift.

Gardener: What gift?

---

[5] Ps. 23:1, KJ.

Architect: The gift you have given to yourself. This gift is your presence in the moment. Be present with yourself in the now, in your thoughts.

Gardener: Does everyone have this feeling of lack?

Architect: You mean lack of resources to start your business?

Gardener: No, what I meant to say is: How do I bust through this fear? How do I change my environment or have a fresh perspective on my life?

Architect: Stop trying to change anything. You want to change or control things, and because you cannot, you permit yourself to harbor a silent rage. Don't get wrapped up in your erratic mind. Use your imagination to make your mind a beautiful place. Take care of your business.

Gardener: What business are we discussing?

Architect: I am discussing your present state of mind. Have you ever been told personally by somebody to mind your own business? Well, you might have felt offended, yes? I have been told to shut up. Well then, this is a literal statement that is often overlooked. What I am saying is this: practicing to command your mind energy, your emotion (energy in motion), is minding your business. Your mind is your business. Practice the principle of a GPS.

Gardener: What?

Architect: Your personal "Global Positioning System." Your imagination is energy positioning frequencies that are in the present now.

Gardener: I am a little confused.

Architect: Settle down and relax. Your present reality is a reflection of your imagination. By doing the exercises in this book, you will experience the flow of energy in your present moment.

Gardener: How does this happen?

Architect: Don't worry about how this happens. Keep in mind the Bible verse I mentioned to you earlier: "The Lord is my Shepherd; I shall not want." When you plug in a location into a GPS, in seconds, you receive a map of your journey. You receive directions, a point of destination, and the approximate time it will take to get to your endpoint. Time is relative and based on various factors during your journey. This is the path you are on to your chosen destination. Now, you can accept it or reject it. It is your design, and yours to enjoy or continue to struggle in your wanting.

Architect: Whenever you feel disconnected from your imagination, remember that you have a map. The collective information in parts 1 and 2 of this book will provide you with ways to change a negative state of mind into a positive one. First, start by practicing the physical exercises and the bedtime meditations daily. Find your own interpretations of the dreams and stories I share with you in part 2.

EXPERIENCE IS BETTER THAN EXPLAINING

A Conversation Between Sifu and a Student

A student of the H. Won Tai Chi Institute asked Sifu, "Where are the circles within the first section of the Classical Yang Family-Style Tai Chi Chuan form?" Obviously, the student was not comprehending what he was practicing. Sifu tried to explain the theory to him, which is almost impossible to understand without personal experience. The student became even more confused. Sifu therefore asked me to show him the first section.

My demonstration was sloppy. Instead of taking my time to execute the moves, I was more interested in showing off. Sifu yelled at me to execute the form correctly while observing my movements. I had a breakthrough. Starting that day, I paid closer attention to details and avoided being consumed by my inner dialogue.

I had felt I needed to convince the student of the circular movements within the form. However, when I took a conscious look at what happened that day, I realized that the whole incident was about me. It was my life being shown. Life itself is art, an ever-present phenomenon of existence.

A Comparison to Keep You on Track

The heart can be compared to an engine in an aircraft. In the cockpit, you deliberately arrange the sensors to monitor the assembly of the engine and wings. Your senses act as the link between your physical and mental selves, similar to how an aircraft follows the commands of a pilot in the cockpit. See your body as a miniature planetary system, a living tabernacle.

Trees that Sway

I absolutely love this image: Picture a meadow with trees that sway and sing a chorus carried by the wind. What an amazing, mind-blowing view that would be. You can only conceive of such an image in a dream, and yet your life is a dream, real in the sense of what you make it to be.

Remember, this book is a guide that offers ideas for you to ponder. As you practice these exercises, pay attention to your inner dialogue. How do these thoughts affect you? What deeper lessons can you take from them? I am sharing with you, the reader, that your mind is your business. Take command and do your best.

Now, let us begin this journey.

SECTION 1: THE 36-DAY CHALLENGE

The purpose of this section is to encourage you to consciously take command of your senses. For maximum result, follow the instructions and descriptions I provide.

1.1
Primary Stance (4-Minute Stance)

The 4-Minute Stance is the preparation for all physical exercises outlined in this book. There are four core principles (CARB) that make up the framework of this standing exercise:

Center yourself to connect the lower and upper parts of your body, coordinating your entire body from the ground up.

Align your body from your head to your feet for total body connection.

Relax to release body tension and limited thoughts.

Balance yourself to execute coordinated and effortless body movements.

These core principles are a working process. Practice is necessary to truly experience them.

Find a comfortable environment. Wear comfortable clothing with minimum heels in your footwear, or be shoeless on the floor or the ground.

Instructions

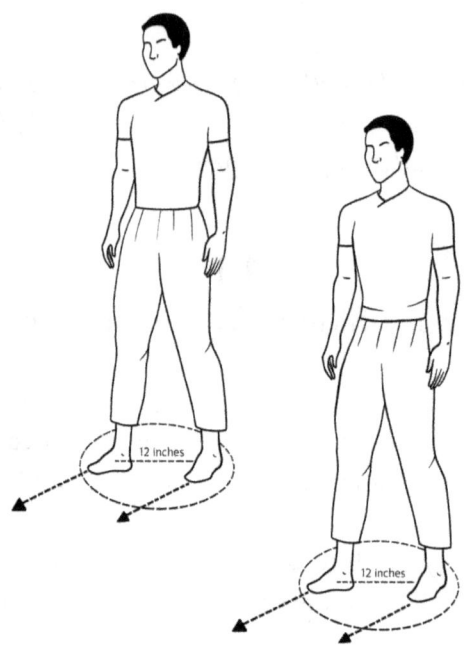

1. Stand with your feet parallel, shoulder-width apart (12 inches).
2. Draw an imaginary circle around your feet.
3. Rock your pelvis forward. This forward movement will point the bottom tip of your spine (the sacrum) toward the center of your circle. Look down at your feet and make any adjustments needed.

4. Your two big toes in front of you are facing 90 degrees, parallel to each other. Your toes, heels, and the outer sides of your feet are solid on the ground, like a book placed on the floor. Focus your attention on your sacrum. This will help you relax your feet.
5. Imagine a light beam connecting your temple body to the heavens through your spinal column, and to the ground through your feet.
6. Hang your hands by your sides with the tips of your thumbs near the outer center of your thighs, and with your fingers alive and relaxed.
7. With your chin slightly tucked in, feel a slight lift at the top part of your neck, like a string pulling the back of your head to the heavens. Keep your neck soft and relaxed, relying on your intention rather than your muscles.
8. Tuck in the tip of your spine at the sacrum. Focus your imaginary light beam through your spine, traveling down behind your knees, and into the heels and sides of your feet.
9. Soften your eyes, face, and mouth. Breathe through your nostrils. If you feel any pressure in your chest, open and close your mouth with your lips barely touching.
10. Focus your attention on the bottom tip of your spine, then visualize the inside of your spine. This trains your mind's eye to look within.
11. Breathe through your nostrils with the tip of your tongue touching your upper palate behind your front teeth. Imagine that your entire lower torso is breathing. Then imagine a light force moving in

and out from your front, your left side, your right side, and your back.
12. Relax the muscles in your face. A Mona Lisa smile will help ease any pressure in your chest, but do not overthink it.
13. Take in the sound of your environment. Feel the buzz in your ears. Feel a sense of quiet inside.
14. Imagine waves of energy spiraling down your spine. Imagine these waves traveling from the womb of the earth, through your feet, up your spine, into the crown of your head, and beyond.
15. Scan your body for proper alignment. Relax as much as you can.

The 4-Minute Stance meditation allows for the free flow of energy between your head and feet with no discomfort in your knees. The goal is to feel alive and know that you are one with everything. Feel how quiet your body's temple becomes.

This guided instruction can in no way replace a teacher-to-student transmission. I suggest you read, take notes, and explore in silence. Go over these instructions again until you internalize them. You are designing new habits that take time to grow roots. Be attentive to your movements. With time and diligence, you will experience a renewed sense of self.

As you progress through your daily practice, you can increase the time by two-minute increments, if you wish. This 4-Minute Stance encourages good habits and serves as a starting point for the rest of the physical exercises. It is also the foundation of the 36-Day Challenge, your personal coach. I hope it will inspire you to self-cultivate your imagination and make your journey a joyful experience.

1.2
13 Joints Exercise

The 13 Joints Exercise is a set of mind-body focus exercises. It means you are taking your time, relaxing in your breathing, and focusing on the provided instructions as you perform these joint movements.

You'll experience how to open the major joints with relaxed muscles. This will prepare your energy to flow, unobstructed. A mindful intention is required to relax your muscles while performing these exercises.

Here is an analogy you can use. See the thirteen joints as thirteen spinning wheels moving your body as one whole. As you move each joint, envision your blood flowing like a river and turning wheels on a riverboat. The thirteen wheels represent your thirteen joints. The purpose of these mind-body focus rotations is to train you to move your body free of muscle tension.

People disregard their major joints until they experience pain, without linking it to their daily routine. The top concern is to eliminate any discomfort.

The 13 Joints Exercise is vital to preparing your body to experience the flow of your power. This will help you with experiencing relaxation, especially during the Sequencing Set in the book. Start your practice now.

Step 1: Navel Area & Lower Back Tapping

The aim of sharing this internal exploration is to support you in feeling your power from the inside out. The center of the feeling is located in your stomach, approximately three inches below your navel. Tai Chi and chi kung practices refer to the power reservoir in your stomach area as "tan tien.". It's similar to an indoor stove that warms up the entire house.

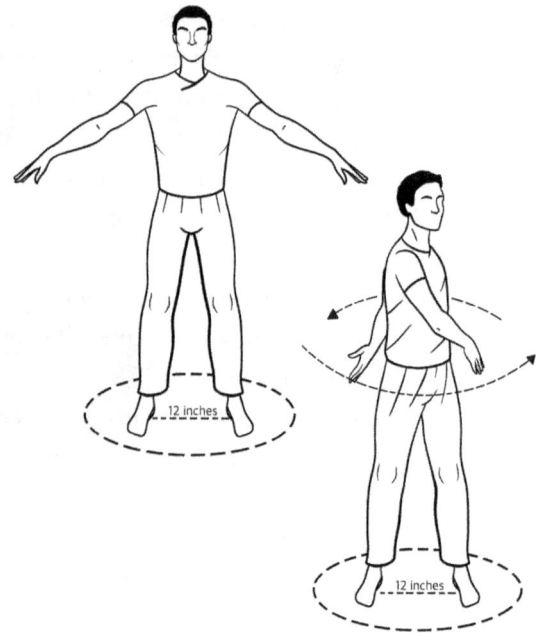

1. Stand erect and relaxed with your feet parallel, 12-inches apart. Refer to the 4-Minute Stance for further clarification.

2. Align your knees with your big toes.
3. Align your hips with your shoulder joints (the "big bones").
4. Hang your hands by your sides with fingers alive and relaxed. The tips of your thumbs should be near the outer center of your thighs, as they were in the Four-Minute Stance.
5. Imagine a light beam pulling from the center of your head into the sky. Then imagine this beam spiraling down through your spine, behind your knees, into your heels and the outer sides of your feet, and into the earth where you stand.
6. Tuck in the tip of your spine at your sacrum. Feel your body where you stand, with your toes relaxed.

    Remember: wherever you stand is always holy ground because this light force passes through your entire holy body, from the heavenly sky to the center of the grounded earth.
7. Raise your arms away from your torso at 45 degrees with palms facing your body. Relax your hands and fingers with your natural breathing.
8. From the center of your tan tien energy, two inches below your navel, begin turning your torso.

    Remember the light force I mentioned earlier? This is a spiraling energy motion, rising up to the heavens and descending into the earth at the same time. In your imagination, your spine gives form to this energy.
9. As you turn, your spinal column is engaged, causing your arms to move in a circular motion. Your left arm swings to your right in front of your body,

touching your navel area with an open palm. Simultaneously, your right arm swings to your back, tapping the lower tip of your spine with the back of your hand.

For reference:

Let us call the area of your navel the front door, and on your back, at the center point between your kidneys, the back door. There is an imaginary internal line leading from your navel to the center of your back.

10. Your shoulders, elbows, wrists, and waist must remain loose and relaxed, giving you a feeling of openness, like sails at sea. Your spine generates this swinging action. Focus your attention on staying relaxed by allowing the momentum of your movement to flow into your arms and hands.
11. As you swing from left to right, glance over your shoulders.

    Start with 24 swings (12 swings on each side). Focus your mind on your shoulders, elbows, wrists, and waist.

Pure magnetic energy manifests as body-mind: a complex network system from your toes to the top of your head and beyond. This whole (your holy temple) is where you live and breathe.

Step 2: Waist Swinging

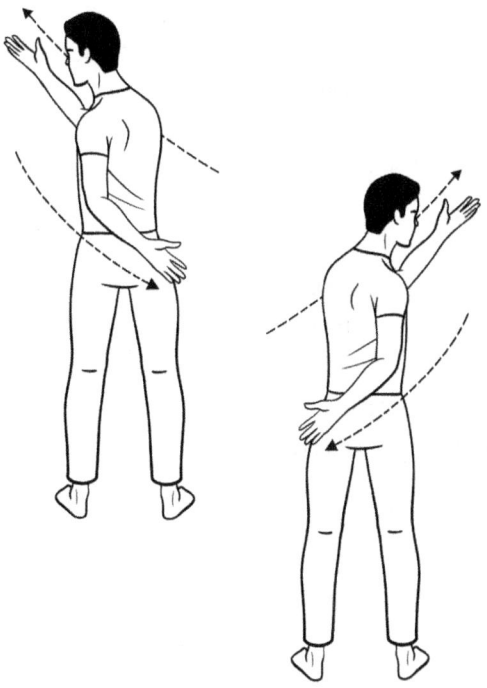

Maintain the same standing posture.

1. Spin your waist to your right and swing out your left arm in front of you at a 45-degree angle, while swinging your opposite (right) hand back, lightly tapping your spine with the back of your hand. Reverse the action.
2. With every reach, imagine a string made of light traveling from your waist, up the side of your body, and projecting through your arms. Feel the energizing lift of this exercise in your hands and fingers.

Feel the internal movements of your waist lifting your arm. Breathe into the fingers of your reaching hand.
3. As you alternate your action between left and right, you might feel a warmth in the palm of your back hand as it taps your spine. If not, don't worry. With practice, you will experience this feeling. Being patient is an invitation from the teacher within.

This meditation exercise symbolizes that you are reaching for what you already have. Use this metaphor to empower yourself. Stay on course. Refuse to give in to any internal clouds or external pressure aiming to break your stride. Relax and set your sails to your desires.

Step 3: Waist/Stepping Forward

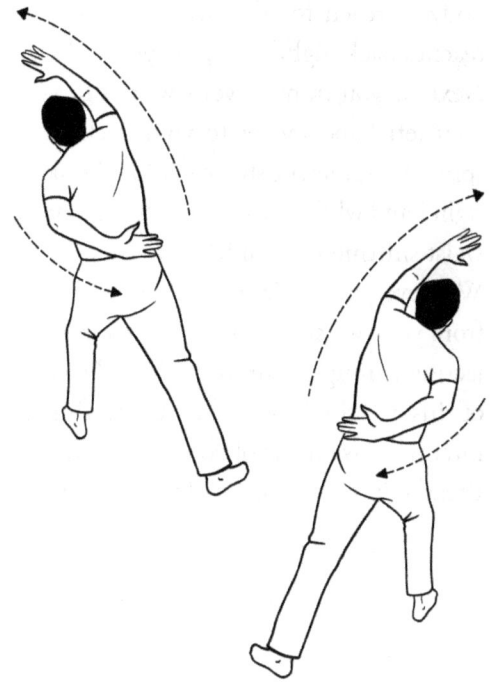

Now that you are comfortable with the 4-Minute Stance and step 2, you now have the crucial tools needed to prevent knee discomfort. You may now move on to step 3.

Start from the position you left off with in step 2:

1. Turn your left foot outward with the big toe facing at 45 degrees, and shift your body weight to your left hip.
2. Step forward with your right foot in a straight line, big toe facing at 90 degrees.

3. Spin your waist as you shift your weight from your left hip to your right. Cross your left arm over your body to reach for the sky, while your right hand reaches back, lightly tapping your spine.
4. Next, as you transfer your weight to your left hip, your left hand moves to your back and taps your spine. Simultaneously, reach for the sky with your right hand while crossing it over in front. Repeat this waist-shifting motion in both directions 12 times.
5. With every reach, imagine a string of light traveling from your waist, up the side of your body, and projecting through your arms. Feel the energizing lift of this exercise in your hands and fingers. Feel the internal movements of your waist lifting your arms. Breathe into the fingers of your reaching hand.

Step 4: Wrists, Elbows, Shoulders, Neck

This next set of exercises may seem simple, but remember, we are training to strengthen our concentration. Focusing on all these joints is a form of personal meditation.

Wrist Joints

The wrist joints connect the hands to the forearm.

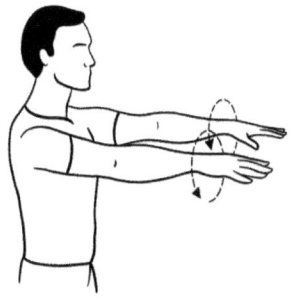

1. Beginning with your primary stance, extend your arms in front of you with your palms facing the floor. Pay attention to your shoulders, relaxing them to reduce tension, and breathe normally.

LOOKING FROM BEHIND YOUR EYES | 43

2. Rotate your wrists joints clockwise 12 times with fingers open and energized. Repeat the motion counterclockwise. Focus your attention on this turning action.

Elbow Joints

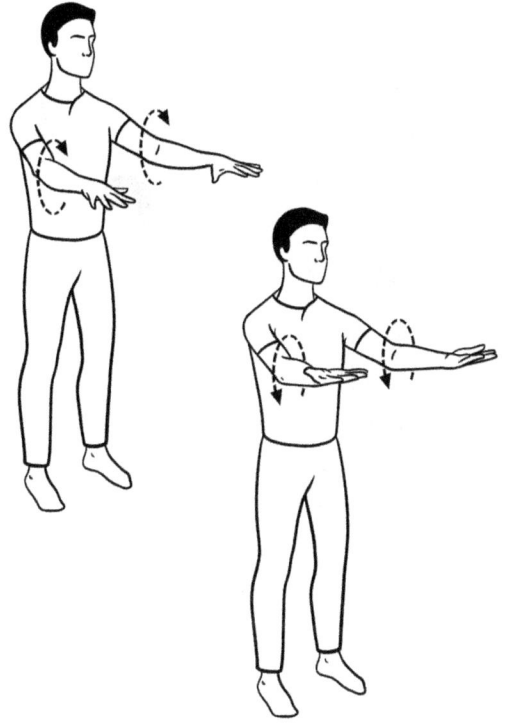

The elbow joints connect the forearm to the upper arm.

1. Bring your attention to your elbows. Relax your shoulders.
2. Rotate your elbows, moving your forearms toward and away from your chest.
3. Visualize two enormous wheels spinning clockwise away from your body on the axis of your elbows.
4. Rotate clockwise 12 times. Repeat counterclockwise.

Shoulders

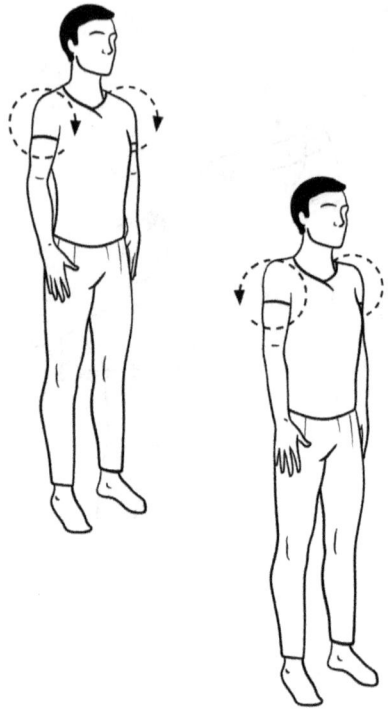

The shoulder joints comprise three bones: the collarbone (clavicle), the shoulder blade (scapula), and the upper arm (humerus). The scapula system attaches two enormous wheels to the upper beam of your temple body.

1. Stay focused and relaxed.
2. Roll your shoulders up and down like two pistons. Imagine there are rotating balls in the center of the upper arm bone, surrounded by ligaments and tendons.

3. Roll your shoulders together clockwise 12 times. Repeat counterclockwise. Feel the sweet spots inside of your shoulders.
4. If you observe your reflection in a mirror while intentionally rolling your shoulders, it will seem like you are raising and lowering them. However, these rotations are all happening inside.

Neck

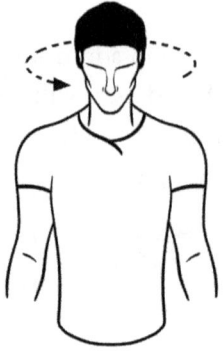

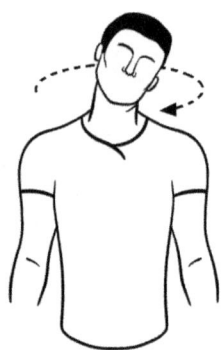

The neck contains muscles, nerves, blood vessels, and the network structure between the head and torso.

Be extremely mindful during this exercise to prevent any discomfort.

1. Relax your neck.
2. Slowly roll your head clockwise 12 times. Repeat counterclockwise.
3. At this level of relaxation, the root of your tongue should feel heavy and free of tension.
4. Once you finish your neck rotations, use your hands to massage the back of your neck.

Step 5: Ankles, Knees, Hips

Ankles

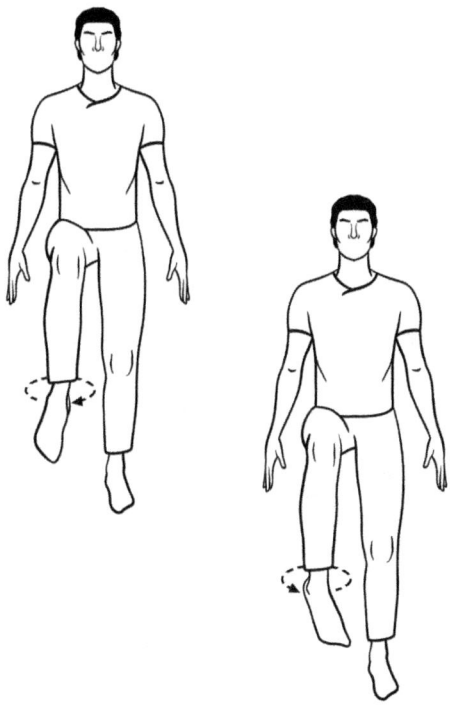

1. Begin at the primary stance, with both feet facing forward.
2. Shift your entire weight to your left hip.
3. Lift your right leg with your knee bent at a right angle (thigh parallel to the floor) and your hip relaxed. If you are having difficulty finding your balance, hold on to a physical object for support, such as the wall.

4. Relax your hands at your sides, fingers open, and palms full of energy. Focus your attention on the bottom tip of your spine.
5. Rotate your right ankle clockwise 12 times.
6. Repeat counterclockwise.
7. Repeat with your other leg.

Knees

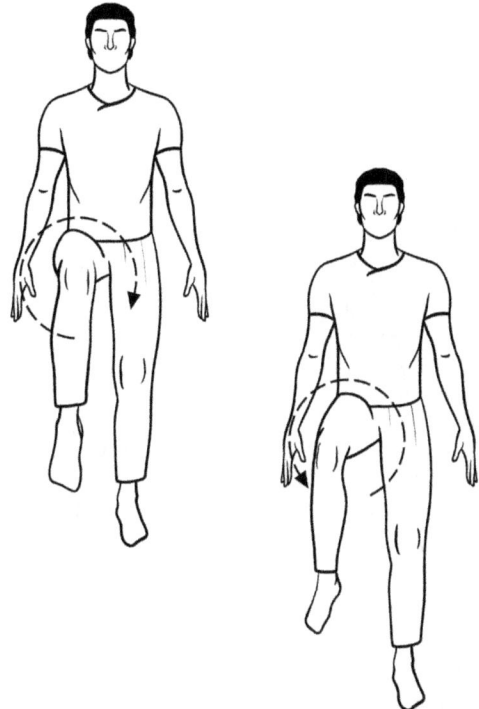

1. In the same posture as the ankles exercise, rotate your right knee clockwise 12 times. Repeat counterclockwise.
2. It should feel like you are swinging your right leg inward and then away from your body without effort or tension.
3. Repeat with your other knee.

Note: See below for more information about the proper care for the knee joints.

Hip Joints

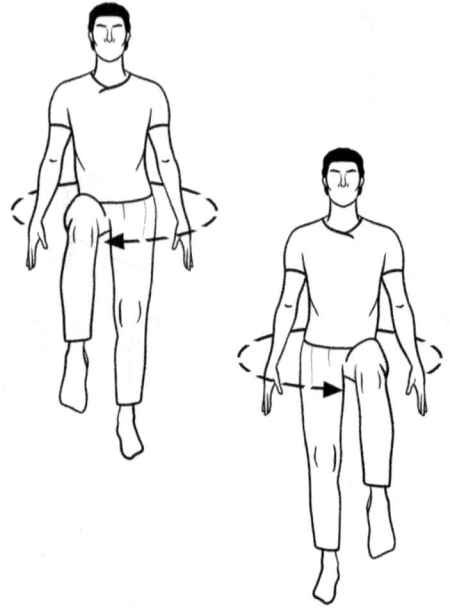

1. In the same posture as the knees exercise, rotate your right hip 24 times by moving your hip from front to back in a circular motion. Imagine a Ferris wheel that is generated from the center.
2. Relax your torso and your shoulders so that there is very little tension. Imagine that the circular motion of your hip is generated by your pure, loving internal energy.
3. Do not rush these movements. The rotation is more mental than physical.

    The opposite rotation is unnecessary to open your sacrum area.
4. Repeat with your other hip.

Stirring The Water

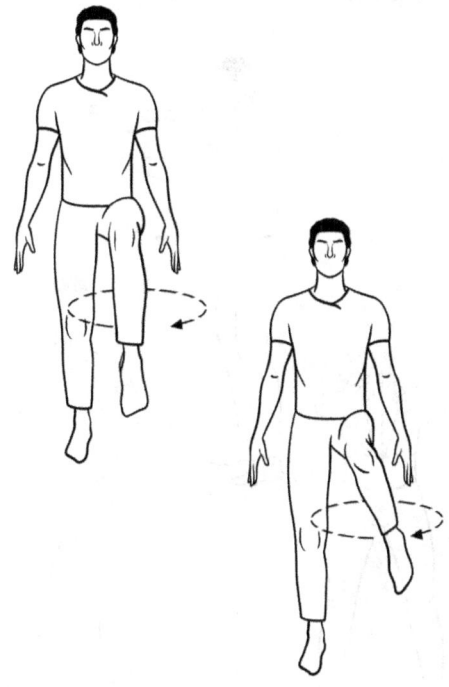

1. After you have become comfortable with the rotations of your ankles, knees, and hips, now we will combine these joints together.
2. Move your knees, ankles, and toes together 12 times in a clockwise circular movement, like stirring water in a round pond.
3. Repeat counterclockwise.
4. Repeat with the other leg: clockwise and counterclockwise.

1.3
Scapular Muscle Engagement

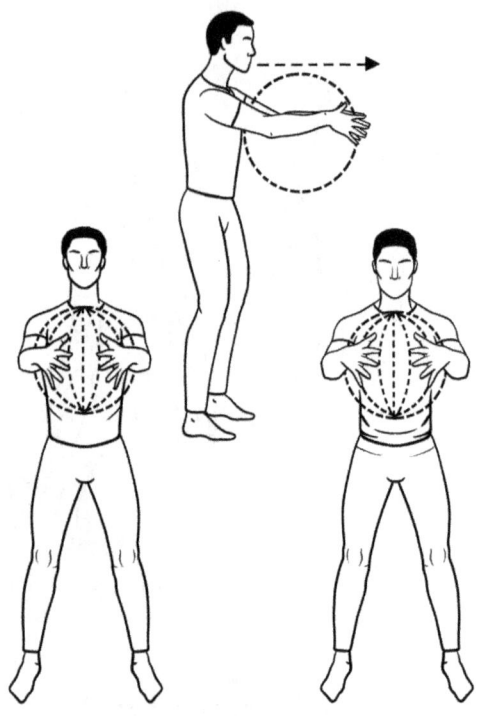

Once you've completed the 13 Joints Exercise, it is good practice to stretch the scapular muscle.

The scapular muscle (upper-back muscle) connects both shoulders.

1. Imagine warping an enormous heavy ball with your scapular. As you hug the ball, sink slightly.
2. Imagine that the ball is breathing into you, shaping your scapular to be round.

3. Slightly sink your sternum inward while you exhale softly. Your scapulae will correspond by forming a curve from your spine at the center of your back. Feel the opening sensation in your shoulder blades.
4. Relax and observe your natural breathing.
5. "Embracing the ball" is a concept that plays a huge part in the fundamental body structural movements of tai chi chuan.

1.4
Pressing Between Walls

After the Scapular Muscle Engagement exercise, it is good practice to straighten your forearms.

1. Extend your arms out at your sides so they are parallel to the floor.
2. Bend your wrists as if the palms of your hands are pushing against two imaginary walls. This gives your fingers, wrists, and elbow ligaments (between your wrists and elbows) a good stretch.

1.5
Eyes Orbiting

"Eyes Orbiting" is a term I invented for myself. Early one morning just before sunrise at Montjuïc mountain in Barcelona, I instinctively started opening and closing my eyes. Then it occurred to me that I had never considered the muscles in my eye sockets during my warm-up routine, so I devised a three-part series of eye movements. I felt more relaxed and connected to myself. Consequently, I include my newfound eye exercises into my daily routine. I hope Eye Orbiting is a valuable addition to your workout.

Temple's Cathedral

1. Get into your primary stance with your feet parallel, shoulder-width apart. Relax your toes, heels, and outer sides of your feet.
2. Imagine your temple body is connected by an energy source. Imagine it traveling through the center of your head, along your spinal column, behind your knees, and down into your heels.
3. Stand at ease with your neck relaxed, looking out at a level position. Open your eyes wide, observing everything in front of you.
4. Keeping your eyes wide open, relax your face. Imagine the image of your face disappearing, leaving only your feelings as a reference that you have a face.
5. Remain relaxed and as still as possible.

6. Take in everything you see in your environment without judgment, observing your thoughts and feelings.
7. Say to yourself, silently, "I am looking from behind my eyes."
8. Repeat this message to yourself, staying as relaxed as possible.
9. Now, shift your awareness to the top of your skull. Imagine your skull from within having a dome shape, like a cathedral. It is your temple's cathedral. Focus your attention there for a minute.

Bicycle Wheel

1. For this next phase, practice outdoors in the open air.
2. Bring your attention inside your head, to your skull's cathedral.
3. Using your mental energy, rotate your eyes 12 times within their sockets, like a bicycle wheel. Observe this circle by looking up into the sky.
4. In the distance, draw a slow, circular-shaped line, starting from the sky and ending down in front of you. Continue this steady flow to the ground beneath you, then up from behind you, and back to where you started. At first, you may realize it is challenging to maintain a steady flow because your mind will rush ahead. Daily practice will bring improvement.

Orbiting the Sun

1. Circle your eyes clockwise 12 times, and then counterclockwise 12 times. I call the circular-shaped line in both directions Orbiting the Sun.
2. Orbit your eyeballs like a Frisbee flying parallel to the sky and the earth.
3. Do the Frisbee fly or the image of a CD (Compact Disc) spinning, 12 times clockwise and repeat counterclockwise.
4. Be engaged in this mindful eye meditation. It is important that you work from an open, joyful heart.

Your reasoning mind may initially reject your practice, so perceive these exercises as a meditation routine to overcome self-rejection. Embrace them and remind yourself that this is your internal observation practice.

Customize these eye exercises and practice them in your own way.

2.1
Four Corners, Four Wheels

First Direction

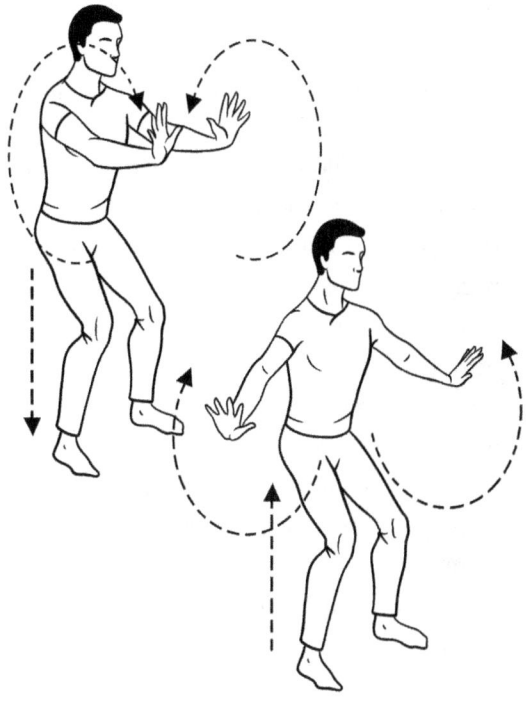

1. Begin in your primary stance, with your feet parallel and shoulder-width apart.
2. Imagine your spine is spiraling from your sacrum up to the base of your skull. As your body moves up and down, rotate your hips and shoulder sockets at the same time.

3. Raise both hands in front of you at chest level, fingers open, with your thumbs two inches away, as if about to clean the imaginary convex mirror in front of you.
4. Relax your shoulders and elbows as they hang at 45 degrees, feeling a force at the base of your palms, or a tingling in your fingers.
5. Move your body down into a squatting position and then back up, the movement of your palms swiping this mirror balloon in an outward circular motion.
6. On the downswing, sit back into your sacrum. On the upswing, allow your spine to lift your body back up to where you started. When you are doing it correctly, it will feel as if you are reaching for the heavens on the upswing.
7. Focus on your heels and the sides of your feet to direct your energy flow behind your knees.
8. Observe your four corners (shoulders and hips) as your spine spirals up and down, keeping your legs as relaxed as possible, so that your spine actually generates the up-and-down motion.
9. As you move up and down, remember to touch the tip of your tongue to your palate behind the upper teeth.
10. Repeat, instead swiping your palms in an inward motion.

Starting Point; Second Direction

Inner Visual Work

While carrying out the Four Corners Exercise, focus your attention on the inside.

Observe your body's motion from within, feeling the flow of sensation through your hands without attaching thoughts of any external stimulation or internal emotions.

Quiet your mind, relax your breath, and direct your energy through your hips. As you lower your torso, direct your weight to the back of your knees, and down into your heels and the sides of your feet. Stay centered, visualizing an imaginary line passing through your body column.

Occasionally, while practicing the Four Corners Exercise, let your imagination run wild.

Here are some ideas to consider:

- Consider that any discomfort or stiffness in your shoulders and hips could be due to emotional residues.
- Think about how your past limited thoughts and beliefs may be affecting your practice.
- Create a beautiful space in your mind by unraveling your judgments. Listen attentively to your soul's voice and trust it.

The more you practice, the better you'll understand moving meditation as a profound experience. Staying present and observing from behind your eyes is at the core of the practice. Experience a feeling of openness and relaxation in your hips.

Family Demonstration

Safety should be a top priority when engaging in any exercise. Now, here is a family story that I hope will inspire you to pay attention and move ahead.

Introducing my family to the 13 Joints Exercise for the first time was eye-opening. I agreed to have a virtual meeting on Zoom with my mother, my sister, and my younger brother to introduce them to the exercises I've shared with you. I showed them the elbows, waist, hips, and knees exercises.

Now, here comes the mind challenge.

I told my mother not to do the exercise that requires squatting, because I felt it could aggravate her knees. She had been receiving medical help on her knees for years.

I showed my sister and brother how to align and center their body. How to direct their weight behind their knees and into the heels of their feet, preventing any pressure from accumulating in the front of their knees during the Four Corners Exercise.

We were unaware that Mom was paying attention to my explanation. Next, I told them to get ready to rock and roll when Mom stepped in line with everyone else.

At that moment, I thought Mom didn't understand, and that she was about to damage her knees. She had been complaining for years about her knees and the difficulty she had while walking without her cane for any length of time. Oh Lord, she might end up in a wheelchair and the family would blame me.

My brother protested. "Sit this one out, Mom, please."

As we already learned, Mom does what she wants. "No" is not an option in her world.

Mom steps in line, engages her core, and opens her wings.

At the end of our family class, she was smiling like a teenager. We had to ask her if she was okay, and of course, she said yes!

My lesson in this act of confidence is to believe in the power of others, which meant I would have to first believe in the practice without doubts.

Paying attention to the little details will take a while, but it is immensely worth your time. Don't pass over them so quickly. I can honestly say that practice will strengthen your belief, and in turn, naturally inspire others.

Our objective is to integrate your four corners (shoulders and hips) into one smooth sequence. Mastering the swing will require time and effort.

2.2
Figure 8

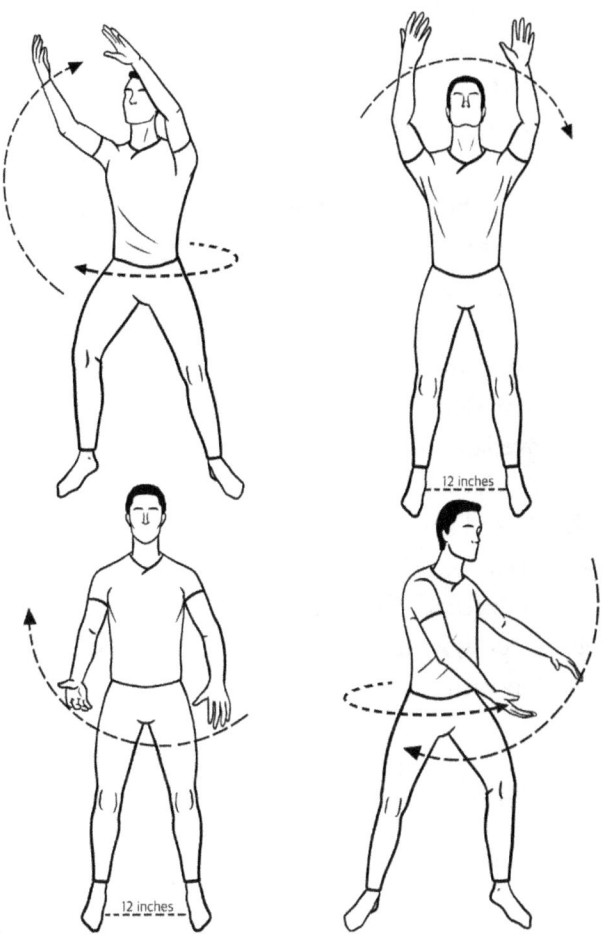

1. Begin with the 4-Minute Stance exercise.
2. Shift your sacrum forward to relax your knees until they are slightly bent.

3. Step forward with your left foot and turn your right foot 45 degrees.
4. Shift your weight to your front (left) foot, your four corners (hips and shoulders) aligned in front at 90 degrees.
5. Relax your shoulders, soften your eyes, and touch the tip of your tongue to your palate behind your top teeth.
6. Raise both hands, with your left palm facing you and right palm facing outward.
7. Spin your spine, shifting your weight from the left foot to your right foot. Use both hands to create two circles, engaging your shoulders and hips to move left to right, back and forth. Both circles will overlap with each other, creating an infinity sign or figure eight. Do this 12 times.
8. As you shift your weight from one foot to another, keep your fingers open and alive with energy, and your feet and toes relaxed on the ground.
9. Repeat, with your right foot in front and with your left turned at 45 degrees.

Practicing the Figure 8

Keep your focus at the center of your sacrum. Use your imagination and observe your spine spiraling as it shifts from hip to hip, starting from your back foot to your front foot. Maintain this focus when you alternate feet. As your spine spirals back and forth from left to right, feel the centrifugal force lifting your arms from the base of your hips and into your fingers.

Imagine that when you lift from your hips, your arms act as wings. This will help you stay in balance and alignment with your four corners.

The key is to be consistent with these exercises and weave them into your daily life. This will assist you with becoming aligned with your well-being. You're taking command of your mind. You're mastering the art of feeling present wherever you are.

Review the exercise instructions for clarity.

It will take time to implement all the details together into one smooth flow. Practice these exercises every day until you experience your infinite self. Once you finish each practice, take the time to scan your body. Are you hunching your shoulders instead of standing grounded in life with your heart open? Are you standing with your head erect with confidence as you express yourself?

How Do You Treat Yourself?

Your body is your broadcast station where the whole "you" is in expression. Get rid of the school of thought that says meditation is some kind of practice with rules and virtues that you need to learn. Learning experiences are desires in action.

Whenever someone says to me they don't know who they are, I remind them they have no obligation or duty to anyone but themselves. There is absolutely no one to please or validate your existence to. No one in higher or lower places can tell you who you are. You may believe otherwise, but only you can feel what you feel. Meditation is your conscious awareness of your daily actions and interactions with your body, mind, and environment.

2.3
How to Properly Care for Your Knees

Have you ever wondered why so many athletes develop knee problems? Coaches often miss that athletes are crouching and putting pressure on their knees with their hands.

If you need to warm up your knees, review the knees exercise in step 4.

I was one of the misguided athletes following the pack. After surviving a knee operation in my twenties, I was fortunate to find a knowledgeable tai chi teacher, Sifu Gim, founder of H. Won Tai Chi Chuan. Within one year of slow, focused, one-on-one instruction from Sifu Gim, a whole new "me" emerged. My knee pain and stiffness from my operation had vanished, leaving only the memory to talk about. I was now walking without limping or pain. Sifu Gim's instructions on how to move required no pressure on the knees.

All practitioners under his direction strictly adhered to the postures and execution within the form. In his words, "Your knees are not designed to carry weight." Establishing your center and body alignment will result in your weight naturally moving behind your knees and into your heels and the sides of your feet.

This practice forever changed my life when I started practicing Tai Chi Chuan and realized the traumatic impact that emotions had on my situation. It surprised me to discover some hidden emotions I had to deal with. I realized this ancient martial art was more of a mental challenge than a physical one when under the guidance of a skillful teacher. Sifu always reminded his students that the mind gives up before the body. He proved it to me several times during the eight years I spent at his school.

If at some point you feel these exercises are too simple, think again. The 36-Day Challenge and other exercises have a psychological impact rather than a physical one. Engaging with these exercises prompt you to pay attention to the position of your feet and prepares your body to direct the flow of energy weight behind your knees.

2.4
Sitting Observation Technique

When you complete your daily exercise routine, it is good practice to end with the Sitting Observation Technique. You can also practice this first thing in the morning. Begin right there, sitting at the edge of your bed—or on a chair or sofa—with your feet on the ground. Practicing this for a few minutes every day will align your nervous system and set your mood for the day.

1. Sit quietly in a comfortable chair.
2. Close your eyes slowly, as if in a drowsy state, allowing yourself to hear every sound in your environment. Be present, without judgment.
3. After a minute, bring attention to your breath.
4. Lightly touch your palate behind your front teeth with the tip of your tongue.
5. Relax your face, then your throat, and then your entire body. Melt away any tension in your shoulders, neck, and chest. If you find it difficult to relax your chest, separate your lips slightly—it will help to release the pressure in your sternum.
6. Notice how smooth your breathing becomes when your body is in this relaxed state.
7. When you are ready, focus your attention on the backs of your eyes while keeping your face, throat, shoulders, and your entire body relaxed.
8. While looking inside the back of your eyes, guide your attention down into the lower section of your stomach and silently say to yourself: "I Am!" Keep

saying these two words over and over, as much as you wish. Practice daily. After a while, this meditation will become natural within you.

The exercises in this book seem simple enough, but they require focus in order to achieve rewarding results. Reread these instructions now and then for clarification.

You can incorporate these exercises as a supplement to the warm-up routine of your preferred sports, or in your daily exercise. I also urge you not to rush through any of these posture exercises.

SECTION 3: MEDITATION AT BEDTIME

If you want to have a say in how tomorrow will unfold for you, it is essential that you prepare yourself for bedtime. You are like a farmer who is about to sow seeds, knowing that he must first prepare the ground. The farmer confidently plants the seeds, knowing nature's elements will nurture them. You must do the same by cleaning your mind of any negative thoughts before sowing your visionary desires. Your dreams can reveal the level of preparation in your conscious and subconscious mind.

Here is an example of a lesson I learned in night school:

In a dream, I shared a Bob Marley quote to a group of Jamaican school children: "I am not on the black man's side or the white man's side but on the side of God, who causes me to come through black and white." I then said that Bob could not share this message with everyone in his circle.

Before I could finish speaking, a young lady in the group said to me, "He felt it deep in his heart where it matters most." That is so true because he often said that God wrote all of his music, which he shared with the world.

I often share Bob Marley's quote with my friends in admiration of the artist. I must confess that it makes me feel proud to know of his music and messages. The dimensional realm of imagination in this night school lesson reminded me that the message of unity is within us all, where it matters most.

The Meditation at Bedtime section can also help if you are having trouble sleeping. Maybe there are some uncomfortable moments in your day that you are struggling to let go of, or you are trying to force something, like wanting to control a situation or holding on to regrets. With daily practice, a natural equalization will occur within you.

3.1
Reverse Meditation before Night School

The Reverse Meditation will help to strengthen your concentration and prepare you for night school. To access this dimension just before going to sleep, review your daily activities in reverse. For example, start with the last thing you did before bed and work your way backward to the first thing you did at the start of the day.

Don't underestimate this exercise by its simplicity. It'll test your mind, so give yourself time to adapt. I asked a friend to practice it, and he later shared with me how hard it was for him to do, as he had difficulty remembering his actions during the day. So, I advised him to review his reversed day in segments of three or four hours rather than through small and detailed activities. Also, if there was an unpleasant incident during your day, think of it as empowering that you overcame it. Then continue with the viewing of your day in reverse.

Occasionally, I will drift off to sleep somewhere in the middle of this exercise. Give yourself a chance to see it through. It's a mental weight-lifting workout without the weights. You may discover for yourself, as I did, that you are becoming more attentive to your daily actions. Have fun with your concentration as you fine-tune this practice, and if any stress or tension comes up, just relax and smile.

3.2
Diaphragm Observation

When you allow your body to breathe normally, you are allowing it to relax. As you progress through the 36-Day Challenge or the 13 Joints Exercise, there is no need to implement a unique breathing technique. Practice internal observation instead.

Here are some simple tips to follow:

1. Bring awareness to your present state.
2. As you inhale, observe your diaphragm, and imagine your abdomen expanding into a round ball on all sides.
3. Remember that your sense of feeling is your guide, reminding you to relieve all the tension that arises in your body.
4. Be present, calm, and steady. As you experience this pure awareness, your physical body will follow the mind.
5. As you inhale and exhale, feel your lower abdomen and slightly contract your anal muscles. Imagine pumping air into a balloon as it fills from the bottom upward.

Remember what it feels like in the 4-Minute Stance. Your inhalation and exhalation must be natural and automatic. Try holding your breath for some time. After a certain point, the built-up pressure within your body will force you to breathe.

If you have the chance to observe a newborn baby breathing, you will see the child's stomach expand. We are born doing this dance, yet as adults, our breathing becomes labored. Over time, the abdominal muscles become weaker and have less energy. Most people are not even aware they're not relaxing in their body's temple.

Here you are doing two distinct internal movements: observing both your abdomen and your anal muscles dancing. I encourage you to cultivate this feeling in your practice. It is for the sake of your life.

3.3
The Observer Technique

1. Lay flat with your spine on the floor or a firm mattress.
2. Bend both knees with your feet flat on the floor. In this position, when your spine is parallel to the floor, it is able to relax.
3. Imagine your back expanding into the balloon shape of your abdomen, with your spine at the center.
4. Relax your open hands at your sides and relax your shoulders.
5. Make yourself comfortable, especially your neck and throat.
6. Relax your abdomen while slightly contracting your anal muscles.

Combine all three bedtime meditations into one practice. If any stress or anxieties arise, just smile and continue practicing. I encourage you to listen to the silent voice within, reminding yourself that this is your life, made with your design.

These bedtime meditations only work if you practice them. When you are able to observe your inner space, you will drift off to sleep effortlessly.

LOOKING WITHOUT JUDGMENT

Let us now continue our exploration into the world of dreams and stories.

Here is a quote about observation from the novel *Mutant Message From Forever* by Marlo Morgan: "Observation is linked to understanding, to knowing the truth that all is in perfect Divine Order, that we as humans are only choosing to live less than our perfection."[6]

Pay attention to how you react to personal situations or events in your daily life. Once you glorify negative feelings, concentrate on something else. Instead of self-judgment or doubt, shift your negative feelings to positive feelings as fast as possible. It's important to clarify that old, repetitive conditioning cannot be neutralized overnight. To shift your state of mind, you need to prepare. To embrace new and empowering states of awareness in life, both body and mind must be tuned and open. It's better to take action in preparation than to react to undesirable states.

The debate isn't about whether your emotions are positive or negative, but which emotion you focus on and amplify. Keep in mind there is no one judging you but you,

---

[6] Marlo Morgan, *Mutant Message From Forever* (New York: Harper Collins,1999), page 120.

yourself. Work toward being subtle with your energy. Pay attention to your thoughts and try to learn from them. You have a range of tools available to assist you with unlocking your ability to cultivate nonjudgmental states.

HONORING THE BODY

Long before I pondered the effects of emotional stress on the body, I was a track-and-field sprinter specializing in the 200 and 400 meters. I took part in high school track and then joined the US Marine Corps track team. Despite loving the sport and training hard, my lack of knowledge about a healthy diet hindered me. I experienced a range of injuries, including knee injuries, foot problems, and even gum inflammation known as gingivitis. Bleeding gums were a common occurrence for me as a sprinter, especially after rigorous track-and-field training.

I later realized that my body was deficient in calcium, causing it to extract this mineral from my gums and other parts of my body. Also, the severe consequences of my low self-esteem were not apparent to me.

Unifying Mind and Body

Your present "now" is a collection of your experiences that you created, so it is impossible to lose anything. The Creative Being within you aims to reunite with its life's purpose. These exercises will help you realize your work here and now. Relax, observe, and feel your way in.

The personal benefits of investing your energy into unifying your mind and body outweigh any other investment.

In fact, this unity will support you throughout your life's journey. When you understand the importance of investing in your well-being, you will move upon this earth with delight. You can go anywhere without worries, exploring your vast imagination with no fear of psychological or physical illness. This is how life should be.

RETIREMENT IS A WASTE

A good friend of mine who retired from his government job of twenty-five years told me that "retirement is not what it's made out to be." Those were his exact words. What I saw in his eyes spoke louder than what he said. His fear of being alone terrified him. I felt compassion for him because he has the financial savings and the time to travel to his favorite Hawaiian island, which he'd once visited.

Before he retired, he spoke to me many times about his dream island. He said, "I will take a trip to the island and stay for a while, and possibly move there after retirement." He now lives alone, with no responsibilities or personal attachments. When I asked him about his dream to travel to this paradise, he said, "Suppose I get sick. The medical facilities on the island are inadequate to take care of my medical needs."

My friend now lives in the big city where he worked in order to maintain his medical policy. He can't afford to give that up for enjoyment because he does not have his health. He invested time and money in his job's medical insurance plan and his IRA investments, but not his personal, psychological, or physical health. The bank account for his personal health is empty.

During the first draft of this book, my friend, while living alone in his apartment, left his body. If you are not investing your time and energy into a lifestyle that supports your needs and desires, you are wasting them.

The Cheerful Investor

The physical and mental exercises shared in this book can empower you to be a good and cheerful investor. Whatever you spend your time and energy on, study it diligently and intend to share it with others. People appreciate those who share their worth in their own style and fashion.

HABITS ARE NOT PERMANENT

It is essential to know that undesirable habits are not permanent, even though your senses may say otherwise. It is not your fault that you harbor these habits, but it is your responsibility to change them. One way to change a habit is to change the way you feel about it. You must be conscious of it and also have a desire to let go of it.

Direct your attention towards something you desire. An illustration of this is learning to play an instrument which can divert your attention from unwanted habits and push you to embrace change. By embracing this method, you can prepare yourself more effectively for upcoming obstacles in your life's path. Here is something worth remembering as you explore new horizons: Feel good about what you are working on. Turn your work into a meditation, and before you realize it, your good feelings will replace the old.

Now, there are religious beliefs in which earthly desires are not good, and one must limit their human needs in order to reach enlightenment. Well, I say: Get rid of those duppy stories and reach for your desires. Your desires come from your own powerful and loving imagination, already available in the creative realm of your being. The higher intelligence seeks entry into your world through your desires. If this wasn't so, then you could never have imagined them.

Use your imagination to maintain a joyful attitude during meditation. The aim of this approach is to ease tension in your expression.

Be at ease with what you are doing. When your mind drifts, bring it back to your silent breathing. By doing this, you are teaching your mind to remain connected with your body.

YOUR FIRST THOUGHT IS A GUT FEELING

Have you heard of the term "gut feeling"? It refers to the feeling that your first thoughts are correct or the nervous sensation that makes your stomach turn when you are in a stressful situation. I'm asking you this question to provide insight into why we began the 13 Joints Exercise with Navel Area Tapping and Waist exercises. The center of your temple is marked by the stomach, the core of your power reservoir. The stomach, in my case, functions as a second brain. This is the reason I felt this way:

Being a sprinter on my high school track-and-field team, I would frequently experience stomach discomfort prior to competitions. Knowing this, I would scout out the nearest toilet beforehand. Moments before competing, I would dash to the toilet, feeling that I needed to unload. The result, always without failure, was just a bag of nervous gas explosions flying out of my rear end. That was my body's way of saying, "Son, we are ready to do battle on the track."

One day, however, I ignored that habit during track-and-field testing at my school's indoor winter track. The coach was recording the sprinting speed in order to form the relay teams for a citywide competition. I was a little nervous, but this was my team's home base, and I was sure I had everything under control.

My first recorded two-hundred-meter sprint felt good. I was relaxed and steady in my body, but I knew I would do better in my second test run, and so in the next race, I let it all go. As I was turning around the curve, feeling beautiful and comfortable, I felt something pop open. That was the real deal, coming out without shame or apology. As soon as I touched the finish line of that second run, I dashed down the stairs like a madman for the toilet. I could hear my coach screaming, "Evan! Where the hell are you going?" That's right, coach. I was going, all right. Full straddle down the stairs to take care of business.

RUSHING FOR THE DEADMAN ROAD

I got this sudden gut feeling that I should stay here.

So, here we are, taking care of our business, telling our temple body new and empowering stories to transmute limitations. The inner conscious being always speaks first, but we never hear it because the noisy sensory world muffles that inner voice. Whenever we can act on our first impulse, miraculous things happen.

Death Road

One weekend, leading to the Fourth of July, I almost died while leaving the Marine Corps base, Camp Lejeune, heading for the Big Apple. The Big Apple (New York City) was party central for wild young marines stationed in North Carolina. It was early Friday morning when I volunteered, along with another marine, to paint the back of the barrack we stayed in. The sergeant at the time was a man of his word, but always looking out for himself. He promised to give us the rest of the day off as soon as we finished painting.

There was a phase in the Marine Corps that I overlooked, which says: "Never volunteer." I thought about it, but I'd already calculated that I could finish the job by 11:00 a.m. and boogie out of town on our first ride to freedom. That meant I would reach New York City in time for a Friday night party. However, all my plans came to a halt. Before I agreed to do the job. The slick-ace sergeant did not tell us he had to leave and get the paint in the morning. Making things worse, he didn't have it available until two o'clock in the afternoon.

I was miserable with myself when all my traveling friends drove off base at the regular dismissed hour of 5:00 p.m., leaving me behind, working in regret. *How am I going to get off this miserable base without a ride?* I thought.

I finished at 6:00 p.m., just before it got too dark. One of my good friends secured a late ride for us without me knowing. While I was in the barrack feeling frustrated, dirty, and tired, my friend burst into the barrack, shouting:

"Come on, let's go! We have fifteen minutes to get to the Soup."

"The Soup" was the name of the parking area on the military base, where all the marines would meet up for carpooling.

"You don't have time to take a shower, just change your T-shirt—let's go!" he shouted again from the other end of the hall.

I jumped up out of my sorry state, pulled on a clean cotton T-shirt, grabbed my travel bag, and ran down the aisle in my military boots and dirty-smelling camouflage trousers. Running like a madman, I punched the barrack door open to freedom. Then I paused and breathed in the night air as if I had been holding my breath for a while.

My friend ahead of me stopped and turned around. "What are you doing?"

"I don't know," I said. "I got this sudden gut feeling that I should stay here."

"It's okay," my good friend said. "It's a crazy weekend, anyway." So, we stayed put on base for the first time on a weekend in a long while.

The following Monday morning, we received shocking news that the driver and owner of the car we were running to catch had crashed on the highway. Two other marines died on the highway that Friday night in North Carolina. The cause of deaths was alcohol-related.

Somehow, in a desperate urge to hop in to that dead man's car, the voice within grabbed my attention. A few more steps and my family would have needed to write my obituary. The night at base camp felt good, free of a noisy NYC concrete jungle to a sensory world with crickets buzzing in the dark.

PART 2

THE ARTIST'S
DREAM PRINCIPLES & IDEAS

In part 1 of this book, I presented a series of physical exercises that encourage you to feel your own life energy. Part 2 is where I share with you the principles and ideas from my personal life.

I want to encourage you to believe in the value of your own dreams and stories. By now, I hope you've come to realize that there is nothing fictional about directing your mind.

Here is a quote from Neville Goddard, a famous mystic teacher, visionary, and author, known for his profound teachings in the 1960s and early 1970s: "Fiction is defined as an imaginary construction which is unreal—as opposed to the truth, or reality. But what is real and what is imaginary when, in a spiritual sense, all existing things are imaginary?"[7] Neville continued, "The world is all that you have imagined it to be, even though you cannot remember when or how you brought it into being."[8]

---

[7] Neville Goddard, "There is No Fiction," *Real Neville*, 1st paragraph, accessed September 19, 2023, https://realneville.com/txt/there_is_no_fiction.htm.

[8] Neville Goddard, "There is No Fiction," *Real Neville*, 6th paragraph, accessed September 19, 2023, https://realneville.com/txt/there_is_no_fiction.htm.

Neville Goddard's statement may appear unrealistic to some people, but I believe it is not the case for you. He spoke about oneness in mind and body and how to actually experience it in your world, so let us feel this oneness together, looking from behind our eyes.

Time to Be Accountable

A very good habit to cultivate is self-honesty. Take the time to be accountable, and have conscious and meaningful conversations with yourself—no one else but you. Ask for a deeper understanding of what you already know about yourself. Be clear on where you are and what you are saying to yourself in your sacred space. If you are not aware that your thoughts generate your experiences, meaning that your internal dialogue frames your reality, you will have a tough time understanding your circumstances.

"Talking to oneself is a habit everyone indulges in. All we can do is control the nature and the direction of our inner conversation," Neville Goddard said.[9] Goddard lectured intensely about our inner conversation and how we can direct it through practice.

Directing Your Thoughts

Here is a quick exercise you can use to focus your attention inwardly from wherever you are. It takes a few seconds to do.

---

[9] Neville Goddard | INNER TALKING Creates Reality (LISTEN EVERYDAY) https://www.youtube.com/watch?v=JI04KKigRAk

1. Look inward from behind your eyes. Focus your attention on your skull (your cathedral) and allow your eyelids to close softly.
2. Breath naturally without effort and relax your face and lips.

Use it as an anchor to remind yourself that you are in command.

Your thoughts are invisible, yet they reveal themselves in your experiences. They are the creative elements of your reality coming from the same source from which all life originated from. You have the gift of choosing to believe whatever you desire. You can assume that you are here to take care of other people's business, but your business is to find yourself and invest in cultivating your energy field.

You alone possess the first-person realization: "I am." Whatever you think you are, you already are.

Take care of your business by becoming self-aware, and practicing to direct your mind. Your silent conversations can only acknowledge the first person within, which is you.

"I am sad, and I am sick. I am happy, and I am healthy."

For example, you desire health, so feel it inside of you. Not in words, because words are usually confirmation of the opposite. Here are two familiar thoughts:

"I am healthy, but I don't feel healthy." Or, "I am rich, but I don't feel productive."

A shift in thoughts about yourself and your circumstances can generate new and empowering feelings. The quickest way I know is to envision something larger than what you see in your present reality. For when you realize you are one mind, then it is pointless trying to change your circumstances in your physical world.

You may ask, "What should I do to get this oneness in mind when there is so much distraction in my world?" The first thing you should know is that the mind is energy—the directing force of your world. Believe in your empowering imagination.

There are countless stories about how to sit still and seek a quiet mind, but few people can experience this state of stillness. There is no need to suffer. Begin by first claiming that you are already in this state, and then observe your reactions.

Your True Nature

Feeling your own imaginary energy field.

Consider this: we all have the potential to share our experiences in the present. It is a fact that the lessons you gained from past experiences did not disappear into a vapor, but are advancing into your future now.

"I am," which is, all beings are traveling through our own designed experiences—constructed societies where the truth may not be obvious. Despite our reasoning mind's denial, the responsibility lies with the individual to prove the above statement right or wrong. You and I are explorers traveling through a cloud of forgetfulness, yet our destiny is to remember who we are.

What makes you happy is the vision, your compass, leading you to your treasure of self-actualization. This is an instinctive feeling that requires your time and attention, and is the initial impulse for you to remember the true nature of who you are. The choices we have in this matter are to either struggle and complain, or find our flow in the game of life.

PREPARING TO WRITE

I got up off my floor-padded bed one Monday morning in early spring, ready to type up my book. But first, I had to prepare myself for my morning meditation routine. I had a lot of work ahead of me. I had just spent three days at home, working online with a book-writing group. This was my first attempt to produce a book. I had prepared myself for this for months.

The group host led us into a meditation that put the participants in an unconscious state, enabling the author to download the book onto paper. Eight hours a day of writing, and yet I didn't know what I had.

Did I waste three days writing bullshit? I had three twelve-by-fourteen-inch sketch pads filled with writing to type up. How was I going to sift through all this? I am not a typist. Did I lose my mind thinking that I was a writer, and that a book would just magically jump out?

I felt sick thinking about how I was going to spend this day. One thing was for sure: I need to prepare myself to face this dilemma. My partner, whom I love very much, believes that I can accomplish my work. I could not let her down.

Knowing I had to get my ass going this morning and do some more writing and typing, I wish I had taken some time to practice my Mavis Beacon typing program. Writing all weekend, aiming for five hundred handwritten words or more within five minutes, was madness. I hit the five hundred mark one time in the entire three days, but I could not make sense of what I had written.

I remember a coworker who once did not recognize his own signature on a document he'd submitted to his supervisor the day before. Now here I am, and I cannot make out a single line on a sheet of five hundred words!

Have I gone mad? I mumbled to myself.

The lesson I learned was to stop trying to copy other people and know that my desire to do things comes from somewhere personal, somewhere inside.

Start exploring what you are feeling. Practice what you know. Be consistent, and you will find your flow. Who you are is bound to rise to the surface.

DEAD MAN'S FACE IN THE MIRROR

> "It is not death a man should fear, but he should fear never beginning to live."
> —Marcus Aurelius

"Evan!"

That was life calling me, waking me up. It was about 3:00 a.m. when I awoke in my New York City home, sweating, and with a terrible feeling that I was going to die. I screamed inside, feeling this minute would be the last time I was in my body. I would not see the sunrise again. My family would find me dead in my bedroom, wondering what happened. *Did he have a heart attack? Or was it suicide?*

My entire life seemed to flash before my eyes and vanish within seconds.

Shaking with anxiety, I jumped up out of bed and dashed for the bathroom mirror, needing to see what was going on. What I saw in the mirror was shocking. A hard shell of a man's face stared back at me with a terrifying look in his eyes, saying, "If you don't stop looking at me like that, I am going to reach out through this mirror, snatch you by the neck, and strangle you."

"Move, damn it!" I stumbled out of the bathroom into the dark hallway, feeling demoralized. I asked myself: "What the hell is going on with me? Is this how death feels?"

Then I heard: "You are not afraid of dying. You are fearful of leaving your body before doing the work. Stop hiding in your self-made cave. Go out and do your job."

Standing there alone, feeling shameful and angry, I chastised myself with regrets burning in my head.

"I have made a fool of myself all these years! Lying to myself and finishing nothing I started!"

"Enough of the bullshit," I said after I finished punishing myself. I had received a swift kick in the ass, wide awake that morning. I felt the lessons deep within, and now I know how to take care of my business. If you ask me what, or whose, voice I'd heard in my head, I would say that it was my father reminding me to stand up and not be afraid. Allow me to explain.

Don't Be Afraid

Before my father left this three-dimensional world, he told me, my sister, and my two younger brothers, "Don't be afraid of doing whatever you want to do."

I forgot his advice for "donkey years"—the Jamaican way of saying many, many years. But I came through the womb once again during that early wake-up call, with a feeling that I needed to slow down and pay attention. Here is what this looks like:

There is an impressive scene in the movie *Kill Bill*, starring Uma Thurman. Her captives buried her alive, underground, in a wooden coffin. Facing death with nobody to rescue her, she slowed down her breathing, quieted her mind, and focused all her attention on one fist. She punched the wooden coffin again and again with a laser-sharp focus, and punched her way out to safety. The brutal training she'd received from her teacher, who had pushed her to go beyond her limitations, now paid off.

As hard as some experiences may seem, there is a lesson to be learned. Our past does not vanish into nothingness, but advances into our present-future. We only have to slow down our lives and draw from the valuable lessons of our past that are embedded within us. Now, as I came through the womb once again, it was time to take my father's words to heart.

I went home to my conscious lover, the creative soul, who will do whatever it has to do to be heard and acknowledged. A reminder that I am the dreamer and the designer of my life.

Creative Lover

The poem below speaks of the lover in every one of us, eager to seize the beauty that life presents. A childlike creativity inside us that craves play and laughter, the one who asked, "Who am I?"

Creative Lover, your right is your life, your soul.
Do you remember why you are here?
The work you need to do is Now.
You are here to build and share your foundation of love and
    prosperity as you wish.
To have all of it—your promises as you remembered them.
Everything is everything, and there are no mistakes.
Knowing you are dreaming every moment of your reality,
Where there are no secrets, only stages of remembering.

YOUR LIFE IS YOUR RIGHT TO LIVE

*Taking ownership of your imaginative
power is a living meditation.*

Here is an internal question I believe everyone asks themself in their lives: "Who Am I?" When asked, it is usually from the standpoint of looking outside of oneself for an answer.

To create a story that matches the question, the mind generates more questions when trying to find an answer. When you mentally ask a question, consciousness addresses the question with another: "What do you want of me?" Your imagination is indicating that your answer is your current emotional state.

The internal answer is: "Whatever you desire to be." Not what you want, but whatever you desire to manifest. To me, the opening sentence of a biblical prayer highlights the distinction between wanting and desiring. "The Lord is my Shepherd; I shall not want." My interpretation is that the "Lord" is the Love frequency within me that serves as a constant "shepherd" guiding force, leaving me with no sense of want. Wanting to be in love implies the absence of it, whereas acknowledging its existence within me, I desire to share it.

Now that the question "Who am I?" has disturbed the vast imaginary ocean within you, there is no turning back. You are the one who is questioning their identity.

Imagine the self as comprising two personalities—the inner and outer person—living together as one being. The physical body is a manifestation of the inner being, which is represented as the outer person.

Your inner being is a loving imagination filled with unlimited resources that manifest as magnetic energy frequencies, which create and direct your physical body.

Fearless Nature Within:

The fearless nature is to experience life instead of waiting for miracles to happen. To quote an anonymous author: "Miracles are for the ignorant who do not understand that life is all there is, the great mystery, a never-ending psychological exploration."[10] You are already in the experience of life, and you are forever connected to your imagination. Even as you read this, are you hesitant to believe it? If you are, have faith in yourself. What makes you feel good about yourself internally? Start indulging in activities that bring you joy and happiness.

Here is another quote from the Bible that is worth reading: "Now faith is the substance of things hoped for, the evidence of things not seen."[11] Allow the things you hope for to resonate within you. It is your imagination, with no evidence of them in your physical reality. Find some quiet

---

[10] Anonymous author.
[11] Heb. 11:1.

time to be with yourself. Become that child again, playing in a make-believe world, having fun without worries.

In the world of free-minded children, everything is blissful regardless of what is happening around them. Remember that you were once a child. Well, you probably have no recollection of what it is like to be a child without worries. Regardless, there is a force within you that never leaves you alone, even when you feel alone.

Say these words to yourself: "I Am." You can only use the "I Am" as "you" in the first person. For instance: "I am safe. I am well. I am feeling good." It is an internal dialogue between you and yourself, a spirit-soul communication that is often not realized in our external reality.

Remember what I said earlier: your experiences do not disappear but advance into your future, and are a part of your present now. The present is your gift.

THE STORY OF DUPPIES

"Tell me the story of the Good and Bad Duppies. Talk about those times."

Where do I begin?

"Begin where you are in your memory right now."

Positive and Negative Duppies

I recall running to the riverbank on my father's farm in Jamaica, the Island in the Sun, eager to relax under the bamboo field near the water. That was a magical place for me.

Tell me!

On one particular occasion, while in my little sacred spot, I dozed off to sleep. When I awoke, the sun had already gone home over the mountain. All alone in the darkness, I suddenly heard a duppy in the brush moving in my direction.

Scared shitless, I ran up the hill for home, or: "I pick up mi foot in a mi han and run fe mi life." –Jamaican dialect called "Patwa."[12] In other words, running as fast as I can with my feet in my hands. I lifted my consciousness and turned my feet into wings.

What do you mean you have to run for your life? And what is a duppy?

Nighttime in Jamaica country towns is duppy time. The Caribbean farming communities give birth to duppies. These are stories about ghosts—the good and bad duppies.

The good duppies are usually family members who have passed on. They reveal themselves to you in dreams, sometimes guiding and helping you in their own ways.

The bad duppies, called "rolling calves," are the ghosts that are not afraid of you. They roam in the pitch-dark of night, looking for you. You dare not walk alone at night on the country road in Jamaica, calling attention to yourself. Rolling calves—cow-like creatures with a long chain attached to an iron ball, stand ready to shatter your nerves.

When it rains just before nightfall, you can sense when a rolling calf is nearby. Your head swells up like an enormous balloon, eyes popping wide open in the thick of night with sweat falling off your face.

You can taste your fear as the unnerving echo beneath your foot makes your entire body tremble. The only way you can outrun a rolling calf is to pick your feet up into your hands and sprint for your life. You feel like two of you in one, fighting to stay alive.

---

[12] Patwa: Jamaican Patois is an English-based creole language with West African, Taino, Irish, Spanish, Hindi, Portuguese, Chinese and German influences.".." https://en.wikipedia.org/wiki/Jamaican_Patois.

If you think I am making this up, take a trip to Jamaica on a pitch-dark country road and prove me wrong, if you dare. You don't have to go anywhere to find out. The rolling calf is present everywhere.

This creature represents the sense of man—rigged with demoralizing stories of fear and superstition. You dare not walk this road alone. Your five senses walk with you, reinforcing the stories you believe by default, which create your reality. When you think you hear something, you imagine the thing that makes you tremble. You can even taste the smell of it when your imagination brings it close to you.

Good or bad, these images are fashioned in such a way to keep societies in a certain state of existence. Rolling calves are the mind's senses sailing on the vast ocean of imagination. The iron ball of the bad duppies is like a guide, a chain of story-links rolling in the dark, forgetting their purpose within dreams and desires.

Recognizing Duppy Stories

Here is how my grandmother dealt with the duppy stories. Whenever she would come across a bogus story, she would often say, "Learn to take bad things and make jokes out of them, or learn to make sense out of nonsense." This was her way of saying not to give energy to foolishness. Her grandchildren would burst into laughter at the way she expressed herself. I didn't know it then, but this is an effective way to relieve the mind of limited hypnosis conditioning.

The following is a story of breaking free from a hypnotic state.

At a courier package warehouse in New York City, I saw two male coworkers in a heated argument. Just as the situation was about to turn violent, one man challenged the other to go outside into an enclosed area behind the building. They were about to engage in physical combat. There was no consideration given to the pouring rain and the inability to reenter once the door was closed. Accepting the challenge, the man burst through the door in a rage. Then, like a movie scribe, some mischievous coworker slammed the door shut before the other mad man could follow. The entire warehouse of coworkers erupted into laughter as they listened to the outsider banging on the door, begging to be rescued from the pouring rain.

When the door was open, the angry individual looked like a defeated wet rooster. Standing at the entrance dredged from the rain, he gazed at his opponent and shook his head. Upon realizing their own idiocy, the two men embraced each other. The laughter of their colleagues broke the hypnotic spell that had held their minds captive.

Feeling Furious and Shameful

I encountered one of the most frightening experiences of the rolling calves as an adult when I was in the demilitarized zone: the Korean Peninsula border mountains region, separating North and South Korea. I was a part of the United States Marine Corps Regiment that was stationed in the mountains for four months of cold-weather training.

One of our artillery units was conducting ground bombing exercises during the day near my unit campsite. I had gotten used to hearing artillery weapons in action, but one particular day, a bomb shook me to my core. I felt shock waves rip from the ground up into my body. The earth beneath me trembled. I was furious with myself for feeling afraid. Then my anger turned to sadness when I could not shake the numbing feeling of helplessness. I thought to myself: "I'm nothing. I could disappear in an instant. I'm just a GI (Government Issue)."

"Why would any human being create such a weapon that can destroy the body in an instant?" I mumbled to myself. I felt empty inside, and confused because I could not make sense of it all. My grandmother's method, of course, could not deal with the intensity of this energy I experienced that day.

I remembered what the Rasta people said in my time growing up in Jamaica: "I and I live forever because there is only oneness, one love, one heart, one destiny."

I said to myself: "I am more than flesh and bones." Something more potent than these rolling calf stories that festered inside of me. Something greater within summons the numbing experience to take a pause and ask: "Who am I? Why am I here?"

Our Own Stories

We can resolve conflicting beliefs by understanding the psychological journey within ourselves.

It is the time to create our own stories that support our vision. We can begin by looking at the stories in our cultures from a different direction and rewrite them within ourselves to reflect our desired vision. In this way, we are taking command, directing our senses, giving ourselves feedback on how we can create, and fine-tuning our own stories.

Your imagination is your connection to your energy source, the Creative Source of all internal and external things—an unlimited reservoir of power available to you. Children express this source of power in their playful and creative nature.

SELF-SABOTAGING

There are cause-and-effect relationships in every aspect of our lives. Every relationship is mind-directed. Whether or not we are aware of it, life is a play, and every act is built upon layers of intertwining minds. The cast members are families, friends, strangers, and imaginary friends or enemies.

People often use these cast members as an excuse to self-sabotage their dreams. For example, a teacher saw in her grade-school-aged student a gift for the fine arts. The student received an invitation to attend an orientation at a prestigious high school specializing in art and music. The teacher gave him a letter to take home to get his mother's signature of approval for him to attend. His mother read the letter and rejected it, saying to her son, "You cannot make money from art. Look at your cousin. He has an art degree, and what is he doing?"

His mother was a single parent with six children. She worked long hours to provide for her family. Her chief concern was that her children could take care of themselves later in life. In fact, she loved her children, but her fear of them not making a living was real for her. At least, that's how it seemed. The fact was, however, her son then doubted his potential, which stopped him from attending the orientation. Of course, his big cousin was not making a living with his art. In fact, he didn't even study art anymore. He was too busy working like everyone else in his family.

For years, the student grew up telling this story to whoever listened, that his mother did not allow him to study the arts. The fact was, he used his mother's rejection as an excuse to cover his own fear of taking action. He wore this fear of failure like a mask. This feeling of unworthiness fostered in him a terrible habit that crippled any vision of a happy life.

The strictest and most patient teacher we have is the one inside. This teacher will provide lessons and demonstrations from different angles to encourage the reluctant student.

NOWHERE TO LOOK BUT INSIDE

The goal is to triumph over any feelings that keep us from having what we desire. This requires honesty to overcome negative thoughts about yourself. You are a spiritual being, and you have a spiritual experience on this planet, fashioned into existence by you.

A reporter once asked Bob Marley: "What are your views about warfare roaming in the Congo and elsewhere?"

Bob seemed annoyed by the question. His answer then was straight to the point. "War is businessmen doing business. That's not my business. My business is music." He was clear about his business. Even in an interview, he did not allow himself to be sucked into other people's agenda.

Most suffering stems from two psychological issues.

If you're in a romantic relationship with demoralizing stories, you will now need to replace them with positive stories that align with your goals and vision. It's easy to rant about social issues or society's problems, but it comes at a cost. My friend, this is not the work you were meant to do.

Understanding our psychological issues is not sufficient. We must take action to replace any behavior that doesn't serve us. See every situation as an experience filled with lessons, and learn from them. Contemplate the good stuff and put your mind to work with your loving imagination.

Keep your personal dreams and desires to yourself—no need to boast. If you do, your mind will bring your insecurities to the surface, and objectify them in your reality as reasons not to pursue your work. You cannot force or convince anyone to accept what you are doing, even with good intentions.

Nourish your mind with wonderful music and read empowering books that encourage you to live. Go within and close the door on your senses that mirror your undesirable situation. Be unassuming in your work. Your desires are the imagination of the Divine Ultimate, the creative force of the universe within you. Your acceptance of this truth is an excellent start to self-awareness.

Warrior Macca: A Love Story

Macca was a mighty warrior in his time beyond time. He lived in an elongated mountain hidden in the clouds, invisible to travelers moving across the wide-open valley below. Every morning, he rose with the sunrise, giving praises to his imagination and dancing his warrior dance—his art of defense. He was fearless in battle, fighting to free the forgetful warriors of ages. He never lost a fight. In his heart, all his encounters were experiences that contributed immensely to his self-awareness. His opponents were not his enemies but sparring partners who significantly sharpened his skills. However, there came a time when he felt the need to share his victories.

Having no one to share his experiences with, he dreamed of a lover. A woman lived at the base of the mountain who was known for her healing medicine and wisdom. She had been observing this warrior, trying to get his attention to no avail. So, she built a cottage in the middle of the valley, painted it in several colors that were bright enough to penetrate the clouds above, and left the door open as a welcoming gesture.

The moment came when Maccabee spotted the cabin in his silent walking meditation. At first he perceived it as a lighthouse on the distant shore until he climbed down from his cloudy mountain.

Realizing what he was seeing, he traveled toward the cabin and walked through the door of his imagination.

Desires are of the divine, living in everyone's imagination. Your desires made manifest are like mature fruits ripened and ready for harvest. The warrior on the mountain realized that the open cabin door beyond the clouds was his desire to share his victories. Your desires are the foundation to making your reality visible.

SATISFACTION IN SHARING

Sharing stories brings a feeling of fulfillment. One day, I attempted to explain to a friend the fundamentals of martial arts using Tai Chi Chuan as an example. Explaining the psychological aspects of my many years of practice, I had to review the basic principles of the Tai Chi form in order to explain it in a way that made sense to my friend. While doing so, my perception of the form changed. From that day forward, my daily practice took on a new level of awareness.

Seeking a more comprehensive understanding of my practice exposed a greater truth. My imagination is the desire of the all-knowing, the one who teaches us through each other, seeking expression.

At the beginning of the Tai Chi Chuan form, the practitioner stands in stillness. I shared this standing in stillness with you through the 4-Minute Stance meditation. The exercise emphasizes mental awareness in the physical movements that connect the whole body between heaven and earth. This is a state of body relaxation and a sense of stillness in the mind. A feeling of wholesomeness from head to foot—a never-ending energy force of potential ready to be expressed.

The mind and body's temple find their roots in the oneness of the creative universe. The awareness of this divine action on a personal level is crucial to the practitioner's experiences. This Creative Source, which I refer to as "divine intelligence," is also the origin of your desire to express yourself.

Spine Spiraling

During one of my morning Tai Chi practices, I recalled a documentary I once saw about tornadoes. A storm researcher concluded the inner center of a tornado is steady, like a spiraling rod, even though the body of it is radically active and destructive. As I took notes on the researcher's explanation, I committed myself during practice to focus within, in my center at the bottom of my spine. I imagined a light beam spiraling up my spine, from the base of my sacrum to my neck. I reminded myself I was not shifting my weight from hip to hip, but spiraling my spine from hip to hip like a tornado, advancing parallel to the ground. Words fail to capture my experience, but I felt both calm and energized, like the eye of a storm, as I moved through a sensory world.

I wish for you to strive to feel whole and energized by whatever resonates with your heart. Give time and attention to some daily actions that generate a sense of peace in your body's temple. A daily practice that supports an ideal image of yourself.

BELIEVING IS TAKING ACTION

I've been longing to recover from my track-and-field injuries. I wanted to keep active without further physical damage, and without the need to compete against anyone.

One day, a good friend invited me to join him at a Tai Chi school in New York City's Chinatown. He wanted me to sign up with him and take lessons together. After two days of trying this art, I protested. "I'm not feeling this! This Tai Chi stuff is not for me."

But he insisted, so I gave it a few days before deciding to reject it.

After my third visit, there was no looking back. The seeds that were planted had already germinated. It was what my soul needed. We trained together at this school for one year and then set out to continue on our own. After a while, I became frustrated with the little I knew about Tai Chi Chuan. I researched information in books and videos, which helped a little, but only kept me looking for even more information. After some time, I found Sifu Gim's school. Subsequently, I embarked on an eight-year training journey with master Sifu Gim in New York City at his no-nonsense school. Throughout my training, I had to explore the depths of my mind and take notes on every aspect. He made sure there was no slacking off under his watch.

One Saturday afternoon in class, as I was practicing a few moves, I drifted away into space. While I was in my world, I heard a quiet voice say, "Come back, Evan!"

When I snapped back into my body and looked around, Sifu was staring me down. He demanded results from all of his students. The joke in class was that "Sifu is a monster with eyes in the back of his head."

RIDER IN THE DREAM

Unification of Spirit, Mind, and Body is the Food that feeds the Soul.

I stood in an open field next to a tree, a distance away from a thick forest. Shortly after I climbed halfway up the tree, I observed a man galloping on horseback at high speed, headed for the forest. I wondered why he was riding so fast. As I looked at the branch to my left, I saw a yellow fruit—the only fruit on the entire tree. I wanted to get closer to find out what kind of fruit it was, but it was difficult to climb the tree any higher. I thought if I jumped to the next branch in sight, I would reach my destination much more easily. But if I could not grip the branch, if I missed, I would fall and could die. Then I realized I was dreaming.

"But I cannot die in my dream," I thought. "I should be able to jump to the next branch with no problem." My senses, however, flooded my mind with doubts. So, I did a little test. If I'm dreaming, and I'm aware that I'm dreaming, I can hit the tree with the back of my hand and I should not feel any pain. I did just that, and my hand hurt. Then I thought to myself: My hand hurt because I have doubts, and deep down, I expected to feel the toughness of the tree against my hand.

As soon as I had this thought, I again saw the same man who rode into the forest. This time he was running away from the woods on foot, with his horse following behind him. *What strange behavior is this?* After he disappeared with his horse, a pack of lions strolled in the same direction.

As they were about to pass the tree I was in, I said to myself again, "I am dreaming, so I am in no danger." I held on to this thought with no doubts.

The entire sight seemed so unreal. The man running away with his horse following him made no sense.

Then I saw another man and a woman who approached the tree's trunk with a welcoming look in their eyes. I climbed down from the tree and greeted them. The woman then pointed up into the tree to inform me that I had left my backpack hanging on an upper limb at the top. With confidence that I could conduct this dream, I thought about reaching for my bag while standing on the ground. The woman then smiled as the top branch lowered in front of me to retrieve my bag. I came to terms with the fact that my dreams are the fabrication of my reality, serving as a gateway to a more profound understanding of my path in life.

My Honest Interpretation

For a deeper dive into dreams, check out a TEDx talk on YouTube about conscious (lucid) dreaming by Habiba Awada. She delivered a passionate talk concerning her experiences with lucid dreaming.

In my honest interpretation, this dream showcased my self-doubts and the idea of life as actors portraying different roles. The rider was flying fast in his sense of pride, yet afraid of his power. Grounded on the earth, the rider felt his power but became overwhelmed by this feeling, as shown by the lions chasing him. It was his uncertainty that lagged him. He knew he was in a dream, but his senses robbed him of his fate to believe in himself.

Without judgment, the dreamer (yours truly) shifted from his thinking to conscious awareness. He now felt the root of his foundation, his field of energy, revealed as the man and woman, yin and yang, standing at the heart of the tree. The warm greetings he received from these two individuals gave him the confidence to embrace his power. He was the fruit hanging on the tree of conscious awareness he was reaching for, yet too timid to receive.

HAVING COMMAND OF THE MIND

Despite our inability to grasp the magnitude of our thoughts, we can still influence our recurring ideas and situations.

In the 13 Joints Exercise, we explore nonjudgmental observation and apply it to our thoughts and surroundings while staying focused. Regular practice can help to master the art of directing the mind. Taking command of your mind requires stepping outside your comfort zone. Allowing your inner voice to guide you is the key to embracing your authentic self.

A Story About Having Command of the Mind

Late one evening, while I walked in my neighborhood, I spotted a man coming toward me with the intention to attack me. That's what I was thinking. I had already formulated a strategy to defeat him. After realizing my erratic behavior, I had a moment of clarity and changed my perception of the man walking toward me. I imagined us meeting and having a friendly chat.

When I went to sleep that night, I relived the drama. This time, I witnessed a young student, who was also a martial artist, charging aggressively with a sword toward my Tai Chi teacher's head.

Seated on the floor with his back toward the sword-bearer, my teacher seemed unconcerned for his own safety. He was engaged in a group conversation with his other students, none of whom seeming to realize what was about to happen.

As I readied myself with my sword, I vowed to protect my teacher. "To defeat the aggressor, I must be better than him. Failure is not an option now!" As we clashed swords, the student fell to the floor.

Feeling proud of my ability to defend my teacher, I stood in place, waiting for a response. There was no response from my teacher. Instead, he stood up, and as he walked past me, he told me to teach the class. As he left the classroom, I was struck by his unresponsive behavior to what had just taken place.

I stood in the middle of the floor, not knowing how to even begin. Now the actual battle had begun. How could I possibly lead the class with the supposedly defeated student looking at me, reflecting my shame?

Shifting My Perception

There was a conflict of two opposing forces waging a psychological war within me. The teacher and the student are identical. The student lacks confidence, while the teacher is authentic and dynamic in handling life situations.

Viewing dreams as a mix of life experiences can improve your daytime observation. No matter how unpleasant or scary your experiences are, there's no judgment or debt to pay. Your angels, the messengers of your life, bring your dreams to you, and these dreams are essentially yourself.

It's common for loving parents to reassure their children that their scary dreams are only nightmares, using phrases such as "Your angels are here to protect you." Events can occur within seconds. The key to learning valuable lessons is to not judge. Failing to do so will cause you to relive those moments in your night dreams or waking dreams. Self-awareness serves as a guiding compass. The dormant self longs to awaken and declare, "I am you."

INTEGRITY IS A VALUABLE PRINCIPLE

When we understand life as a culmination of unique experiences, we can then see your failures as successes in reverse. Converting negative emotions into positive energy requires mental and sometimes physical action. Avoid getting caught up in negative feelings, as they can multiply. When you seek the origin of your thoughts, your mind searches through your experiences and memories for causes. Sometimes I just say, "No!" to break the spell before a full-blown story takes control of my body. Remember, your aim is to harness the power of your mind.

Grandmother's Wisdom

My grandmother was a master of shifting energy. She resided in Jamaica, amid mountains in a small country village. During the time I lived with her, I would occasionally hear her chasing away unwanted energy from her yard, mostly in the middle of the day. She would walk out of her detached wood-fire kitchen into the open space, and shout to banish the negative duppy energy off her property.

"Get out of here!" she would announce.

As a child, it seemed comical to me, but now I know this was her way of keeping order and integrity within herself and in her home.

Integrity

Integrity is a highly valued principle. Webster's dictionary defines "integrity" as: "Firm adherence to a code of especially moral or artistic values."[13] It takes courage and perseverance to be in tune with your thoughts and feelings. It is essential to understand the importance of following your desires. Despite appearances, you're not alone in your journey toward self-reliance.

Remove your shoes and show respect for this sacred inner space. Your thoughts will manifest your own personal heaven on earth. Go beyond your current reality, regardless of what it is. Your thoughts reflect your words and perceptions.

---

[13] *Merriam-Webster Dictionary Online*, s.v. "Integrity," accessed September 19, 2023, https://www.merriam-webster.com/dictionary/integrity.

I CAN FORGIVE, BUT I WILL NEVER FORGET

When someone says, "I can forgive, but I won't forget," they often assert proudly: "Forgetting is not an option, so it will never happen." I remind them they are keeping their fears alive in their reality. My suggestion is to forgive and forget. It is tough to let go of hurtful experiences, yet this is necessary to create room for new and pleasant feelings. Our thoughts shape our experiences.

A Tale of Forgiveness

The best example of forgiveness I've heard is from a story about an anonymous Tibetan monk:

"If you watch a newscast about a man who massacred a group of women and children in a community, forgive the man who did the killing. Also, forgive all the victims, forgive the people who broadcast the incident, and forgive yourself, the observer of the newscast."

Forgiveness can be hard to comprehend when our focus is on self-pity or protecting others. The first step toward psychological well-being is to recognize how we are all connected to everyone and everything. The question that we can truthfully ask is: Who am I forgiving? When dealing with forgiveness, you must consider two aspects: Forgive and Forget.

Forgive and Forget

Forgiving and forgetting requires a radical transformation, like a chicken breaking free from its shell and entering a vast open space. A personal rupture, a sudden change in perspective from self-contained to a larger life mission. This realization held me responsible for forgiving myself.

I forgave and forgot feeling judged by aligning myself with the greater good of humanity. Through abstaining from judgment, I learned that I create my subjective reality.

At first, it was difficult to accept that everyone is playing a role, reflecting and rewarding each other like a boomerang. Overcoming self-pity and negative thoughts about others was the biggest challenge I faced in improving my health, finances, and relationships.

Embracing Your Truth

The key to forgiveness is to embrace your true self and acknowledge the emotional state you are experiencing. Reflect on whether you're feeling down or need some inspiration. Find peace within yourself, despite your turbulent thoughts. For example, to forgive entails letting go of thoughts about a victim, a perpetrator; and you, the observer. The roles reflect the dreamer's illusionary belief in people's societal roles. Open the door wide and remove the cobwebs from your doorway. Remove the mental drapes and accept the light that is meant for you.

Our capacity to imagine is what brings us together in oneness.

JOURNEY OF SELF-DISCOVERY

Life's expression is founded on love,
a universal journey of remembrance.

Life dramas are a product of the countless experiences occurring in our inner and outer self. The outer self seeks to discover its life purpose, while the inner self yearns for manifestation and possesses all knowledge. Feelings of doubt, condemnation, and spiritual debts often suffocate the outer self.

During my childhood, I frequently heard the phrase, "The Lord is my Shepherd; I shall not want," repeated in church. I never got an explanation for what it meant. Even today, I think many people are clueless because the question "Why shouldn't I want to?" has gone unanswered.

Going to church on Sundays during my childhood in Jamaica was a painful experience. Sitting on an uncomfortable wooden bench, listening to a baffling, mad preacher condemning sinners, made me feel nauseous. The notion of being disconnected from a mighty god filled me with anger. It left me pondering how a loving god could both create me and threaten to condemn me to eternal hellfire for not knowing how to behave. According to the preacher, the only means of saving me was to allow myself to be dipped in water by a minister of fate. This idea seemed crazy and didn't feel right to me. The religious teachings had a significant and detrimental effect on my mind.

I remember feeling frightened after reading the Bible's Book of Revelations alone for the first time. I felt overwhelmed by the hellish images and believed there was no hope of salvation. So, I made a wish: "I wish I had never heard of this God above and never gained the ability to read."

My reasoning was, if I had lived in the mountains, far away from people, and had never heard of this dreadful god, I would be free from condemnation. The day of liberation arrived when I left Jamaica and reunited with my mother in the United States.

One day, I stood in the kitchen and announced to her, "I don't enjoy going to church." In a desperate voice, I said, "Mom, don't even think of sending me to church."

She must have felt something, because she never asked why. She just looked at me and said, "Okay."

"Yes," I said silently to myself. "My mother is god, the caring god that understands."

Some people unintentionally hinder their own success today. The weight of psychological burdens, rooted in generational beliefs, keeps them imprisoned in a world of debt. Certain regions of the world refer to this debt as "karma." There are various interpretations of this term, but I find this definition fitting: "The consequence of one's actions."

If you feel you need to tend to some issues in a past life, let go of such beliefs today and begin your journey of self-discovery. Focus on you. Imagine your small victories in order to explore life's beauty. Be true to yourself as you navigate through your universe.

CLAIM OWNERSHIP OF YOUR POWER

I was fortunate to have a granduncle in my life who was self-aware. Granduncle Edgar was a peaceful and loving man. I never witnessed him angry nor heard any tale of him being mischievous. He always had a smile on his face, which made him beloved by the children in the community. Laughter filled the yard whenever he was there, especially when he and my grandmother talked about the Rastafarian way of life. We would laugh with our granduncle while grandmother wallowed in frustration, trying to convince him that the Christian religion is the right way to live.

The Rastafarian lifestyle I knew during my childhood is a nature-oriented way of living, rather than a religious doctrine. Granduncle Edgar based all his reasoning on the concept of "One Love." He delivered his words amusingly. As they say on the islands, he practiced what he preached. He closed his shoe-repair business to assist my mother in caring for my disabled father. With an open heart, he answered the call and delivered his service.

Following my father's departure from the three-dimensional realm, my grandmother called upon my siblings and me to move to her residence. Our mother, like most women from the islands, was working as a domestic worker in the United States to provide for her family back home.

Like my granduncle, my father was a selfless individual. As he lay dying, he learned about the recruitment campaign for women to work in American households. He pressured my mother to go, despite the possibility that he might never see her again. He was free in his heart. And as you probably already guessed, they never saw each other again. Three months after my mother went to the United States, he made his transition.

Moving to the United States was a big change for my family. It was difficult for me to leave our father's land, as I hoped to remain at home with Granduncle Edgar, where I felt secure. However, tribal heads made the rules.

What seems like a sad chapter in my life was the starting point of my curiosity. I wanted to gain more insight into myself, my values, and my attitude toward life. I already knew that no one dies because my father told me so. He spent the last three years making sure we understood this truth. He never sought self-pity, as far as I could tell. Despite being in terrible pain, he never lost his smile until the very end. He was a master of his own right.

Feelings of the Heart

"What is life?" I asked Granduncle Edgar. "Teach me about Rasta."

He smiled and replied in a gentle voice, "You are not ready to know yet."

I was only eleven. We didn't talk about it again until I was eighteen and living in the United States with my family.

During a family trip to Jamaica, my brothers, cousins, and I sat around a dining table listening to Granduncle Edgar share his life stories.

In the middle of the storytelling session, he reminded me of the question I had asked him seven years before. He said, "You remember the question you asked me? Now your eyes reveal the answer." He continued, "Rasta is the feeling of the heart. Growing your locks (long, twisted hair) is not mandatory, but if you choose to do so, do it for righteousness. If you don't, it will drive you mad."

I didn't comprehend what he was saying. In the later stages of my journey, I grasped the significance of spending years seeking validation from others for my true self. To the best of my recollection, this was the last and only discussion we had about Rastafari. His way of living revealed everything he could have said later about the subject.

I wrote a poem that portrays how I see Rasta through Uncle Edgar's lifestyle.

Rasta Way of Living

Rasta is a guide, a way of thinking,
A compass at my feet, a function of the heart,
In understanding the human Construct,
The Spell, objectified into the Dream of the Planet.
An invisible portal, harnessing the illusion of race, separation, and limitation.
Feel the Truth, the Truth of Self.
Feel it. Touch the ground, touch the trees.
Drink in the sunlight. Breathe respectfully. Exhale with a smile.
When you feel at ease, Give Thanks and share the Oneness,
In all your talking, and in all your walking.

—Evan Worldwind

MR. & MRS. LOVER LOVERS

Can I tell you about the two loves of my life? In Jamaica, one afternoon when I was ten, I sat on the living-room floor and leaned against my father's bedroom door, listening to someone mourning.

I wondered, *Is my father crying?* I wanted to see what was happening, but strangers inside denied me entry. My father was bedridden. He could not get out of bed without help. My family never knew what happened to him.

I often wondered how such a tall, powerful man could not be able to walk. He was my god. I looked up to him for love and wisdom. He never raised a hand against us, and he loved my mother. Children are knowledgeable about this, you know! "Love me mother su till," is the Jamaican way of saying it. He would do whatever it took to make her happy.

This love story is a little rough, so brace yourself.

My mother came home one day from a crossroads (a junction of three districts) near our home with tears in her eyes. She announced to my father that a man had disrespected her. How he disrespected her, I was never told.

In this mountain country, people handle their own affairs. My father, a respected community member, couldn't stay at home and ignore this situation. He had to represent, if you know what I mean. Being the loving king, it was his duty to defend his empress's honor. So, naturally, he went to the street with his hunting rifle to search for the offender. Can you imagine what the townspeople were thinking, seeing this strapping six-foot-tall man stepping hard with a hunting rifle?

"When that tear-up-minded man saw my father, he picked his feet up in his hands and ran for his life." That's the Jamaican way of saying that he scared the shit out of that man.

Hours later, after my father returned home, a police car drove up and parked outside of our home. We stood on the veranda, observing, while the King talked to the two police officers. They did not arrest him, but they took his rifle and drove off. According to the King, the police officers said he could pick up his weapon at the station after he calmed down. Later one afternoon, my father caught up with the fugitive. According to the townspeople, my father threw the man onto the asphalt and smashed his face into the street.

Let me clarify, violence is not the way forward. I'm only sharing with you the love story of a king the way the townspeople told it. My father never talked to us about the incident.

I also forgot to mention, this king's name was Daniel Ezekiel. The village people knew him as Dan the Breeze. The word was: Don't mess with Dan the Breeze's wife. He received that name because of his renown as a fast driver on the rough country road. At home we called him D, and our mother Miss Datty.

This father and husband laughed all the time, unless he came home tipsy. Alcohol made him sad. He would say "Hmm" and go to bed. Whatever his reasons were for getting drunk, I don't know. All I can say is, there are many ways to address these private conversations. I think he was ashamed of coming home drunk and having to face his family. Now, as I wondered what was happening, I believe those people who didn't want me to enter my father's bedroom were trying to protect me from the sight of death.

MOTHER'S TEACHINGS

After my father passed, my sister, brothers, and I lived with our grandmother and reunited with our mother in New York City shortly after. Our mother developed a system based on her upbringing, which was very effective for her in guiding her four children. She was a disciplinarian. If she called us twice and received no response, we were in trouble. However, her love and creative ways of doing things gave us strength. She knew what she wanted without being loud.

I remember one particular incident when she took my sister and me to register at the community school. The principal of this junior grade school thought he could manage my mother with his intellect. Therefore, he kept insisting that my sister and I would have to be placed in a lower grade. He explained that the American system was more advanced and, therefore, superseded the foreign school systems. My mother ignored his argument and told him the grade level she wished to have us in. After several arguments trying to convince her, the principal caved in to his big armchair and surrendered to my mother's demands.

During this conversation, not once did my mother raise her voice higher than when she spoke. She tolerated his nonsense. In her mind, there was no compromising her intention to ensure her children start school in the correct grade. No amount of training could deliver such a flawless performance. My mother's attention was laser sharp.

Living in a fast city, in a neighborhood plagued with drugs, gangs, and infections, she had to root us in storytelling. She would recite us stories told to her by her mother and grandmother, and about her own experiences living in the United States. My mother taught me there is power in the stillness of mind.

Here are three pieces of advice from Miss Datty to her children:

1. Never lower your eyes to another.
2. Conduct yourself respectfully.
3. Make the bed and put on clean underwear before leaving home.

To her, if you lower your eyes when talking to someone, you lose your power to represent yourself and allow others to look down on you. It was all about holding your stand. She would also say, "Don't start a fight, but if it comes to you, finish it."

Conducting ourselves with respect was a big one for her. She would remind us how important this was. According to her, respect is a universal language.

I believe that was what my mother was saying. Self-respect helps you understand that people across the world are similar in their needs and expressions.

Making our bed and wearing clean underwear, we held as a family honor. We didn't dare overlook it. She often said that in case something unexpected happens to us and somebody has to take us home, or if, God forbid, any of us wind up in the hospital, we wouldn't embarrass her.

My parents' way of saying and doing things gave me strength and remained with me all these years. I am sure you can relate to them.

CLEARING FOR NEW EXPLORATIONS

On the day of my father's funeral, a schoolteacher from the district got annoyed with my brothers and me while we were covering our father's casket with soil. I heard her comment to a neighbor standing next to her, "These children don't love their father. How can they cover their father's coffin without a tear in their eyes?"

She was the same hypocrite who came to the house begging my father to repent. "Master Dan," she begged. "Please, allow me to help you save your soul."

The King did not pay her any mind. He had his own ideas about death.

Our father had prepared us masterfully for his departure. His words to his children were: "The body dies, but the spirit lives on. I'll be here watching and protecting all four of you. Remember this: Never be afraid to do whatever you want to do."

We were all prepared for his passing. He had many conversations with us about death and what it meant to him. I knew my father loved us, and that he would never lie. He was a magician, keeping the fire in our eyes blazing bright, even during his last days on earth when he could barely speak anymore.

Midnight Magic

Prior to my father falling ill, my parents would get up in the middle of the night and create a Parisian café atmosphere in our kitchen. Late at night between 3:00 a.m. and 4:00 a.m., under a kerosene lamp, my mother would prepare some chocolate tea, fried dumplings, and codfish dishes for their romantic conversations.

They filled the nights in the mountains with activity. No streetlights were available in those days, just the dark, star-filled sky above and fireflies buzzing around in the bushes. The moment we detected the aroma from their delights, which fluttered across our noses in the bedroom, my sister, two brothers, and I would make our way to the kitchen in our pajamas.

On some nights, they would wake us up and take us for a night trip on the country road. Driving on the night country road full of duppies was always a scary and exciting experience. All four of us would be in the back seat weaving from side to side, listening to the romantic stories of two lovers.

Create a beautiful mental space for yourself and your family. Imprint your stories on the canvas of your heart to refresh yourself in times of need. It is a noble first cause for the healing of families and nations.

KEEP YOUR HANDS UP

Every child born to this planet has the power within to overcome adversity. This internal power seeks balance within the human temple. It is a divine reservoir of resources ready for expression.

My parents' example of a loving relationship was all I needed to recover from life-threatening pneumonia.

When I was about nine years old, I was suddenly bedridden with a high fever. My mother covered my entire body with grandma's preservatives—a sacred liquid of herbal blends. She then wrapped my aching body with layers of sheets and assured me I would be fine in the morning.

Drenched in water from the herbal bath, feeling completely drained of strength, I perceived a huge planet protruding through the ceiling, aiming for my head. This earth-like planet was moving slowly, destined to crush me and the bed. I felt I was all alone and that no one was there to help me, even though my mother and father were in their room next door.

My mother must have heard me crying. She came into the room and sat next to me in the dark. "Don't worry, you will feel better in the morning."

I took her words to heart and bore the pain. Somehow, I must stop that gigantic planet-like ball from reaching my body. It was coming down upon me for sure, so I raised both weary hands above my face in the air and kept them there. Holding on to my mother's words gave me strength. I wanted to stay alive.

My father showed us every day with his illness that he never gave up. He and my mother were my mentors to fight this monster aiming for me. I cried. I will bear the pain in my shoulders and keep my hands in the air. As I felt the weight pressing down into my hands, and the wailing pain in my shoulders increased, tears ran down my face while my body burned from the fever.

Keep Your Hands in the Air, Joshua

Extremely exhausted, I remembered the church minister in my district preaching one Sunday morning about the prophet Joshua. The prophet commanded the seven priests, who bore seven trumpets made of ram's horn, to blow down the walls of Jericho. In my mind, Joshua kept his hands up in the air for seven days. I thought to myself: he never once lowered them for a moment. I believed that if he did lower his arms, the seven priests would not have had the power to crush the walls of Jericho. He never gave up, so neither would I.

As my arms burned with pain from the weight, I closed my eyes in tears and imagined myself to be Joshua the prophet. My final thought was: *I will stay alive, I will not lower my hands.* Then I stepped inside of myself and disappeared.

At sunrise, I awoke feeling exhausted and free from the fever. This was not a dream. It was real. I felt the love of my mother and my father. Their love never left me alone. This love is forever present and growing. I honored their love that night by doing my best.

You are the one, the power, remembering who you are. This potential force manifests itself in different ways. You know that you, and only you, can do what you do. You are the one loving you, I tell you. Remember this, because You Are. The weight of your experiences may be overwhelming, yet you can always shift your awareness whenever you wish.

Our childhood experiences are forever a continuation of our generational journey, advancing into the future—a blueprint of who we are as artist dreamers.

PSYCHIC SELF-IMPRISONMENT

Here is a story I heard about the great Harry Houdini that illustrates self-imprisonment. Harry Houdini (1874) was the illusionist who trapped himself inside of a locked jail cell. The builders and media reporters invited him to test his ability on a new jail-cell lock constructed in the British Isles, which was thought to be unbreakable or unpickable. He walked into the prison cell, beaming with confidence. After all, he was the master lock picker. A whole hour went by with no success. After being drenched in sweat, he collapsed against the cell door, causing it to swing open. Amid all the excitement, the guard forgot to lock the iron door.

Regardless of whether this story is true, it illustrates how we imprison ourselves in our thinking. Houdini believed the cell gate was secure. Everyone around him informed him that the cell gate was locked, and he believed them.

We always have the power to take charge and guide our own minds. Paying attention to minor details will help you maintain self-awareness despite external factors.

Be smart about practicing your craft and it will remind you to be "you" in any environment. Make your daily practice a meditation. Whether you have twenty minutes or forty minutes, or if you are feeling high or low, find your center and breathe into it. Psychic freedom is a moral challenge because it requires honesty and ownership of your creative expressions.

AMPLIFICATION OF THOUGHTS

When you acknowledge the work you've done for yourself, don't become puffed up with pride about it. Keep this work to yourself.

There is a verse in the Bible that states: "When thou prayest, enter into thy closet, and when thou hast shut thy door, pray to thy Father which is in secret; and thy Father which seeth in secret shall reward thee openly."[14] This prayer is not about broadcasting or begging, but about claiming your true identity as a spiritual being experiencing what you have imagined.

We frequently use the phrases, *I am sick, I am sad, I am right*, without realizing how powerful these thoughts are. It's possible for people to express happiness while not feeling content. Merely wanting happiness is insufficient if negative thoughts dominate. The ability to disconnect from judgment and self-doubt is a skill that requires practice. Embrace managing yourself. Embark on a precise plan to sharpen your senses. Your senses, the executives of your business, will come to terms with your true self.

There is a story about Jesus Christ, where he slept among thieves without being harmed. He lay down his temple and

---

[14] Matt. 6:6.

rose into the higher dimensions, where no thieves could reach to rob him. We can understand the story as a lesson on the importance of a clear mind before sleep. Our regrets, disappointments, or unwillingness to forgive will be the thieves that rob us. Trust the source of your energy account and declutter your mind before the sun sets.

Keep in Mind

Whenever you encounter something that offends your senses, bless it and imagine it to be a pleasant experience instead. If you persist in judging what you see, hear, smell, and touch, your thieves will keep robbing you of your greatest gift. To access your wholesomeness and make changes, daily practice is a must. Keep in mind that you are the cause, and the architect of your reality in the world of senses.

Seeking a Clear Path

Embrace the concept of already living a healthy lifestyle to maintain good health. Feel a connection with your future life in the here and now.

Imagine yourself wandering through an unexplored forest, where you're solely responsible for finding the trail. To reveal the existing path, you may need a machete to clear the obstructing brush in your sight. Realize that you are a living spirit being, experiencing human life within the dream of the planet. Embrace your artistic side and take command of your life as its director, engaged and present in every moment.

Fear is often a result of lacking understanding or trust in the gift of life, and can be seen as False Evidence Appearing Real, or Feeling Excited And Ready. Use the acronym that works best for you. Whenever I share FEAR (Feeling Excited And Ready) with people, it never fails to make them laugh. Does the second definition of FEAR make your heart lighter? I hope it does. Transform your fears into energy for your primary venture, which is to stay focused on the present.

THE CHALLENGE OF EMPOWERMENT

Create a sense of wellness for yourself. Feeling good may be a challenge, but those are the moments when you're encouraged to slow down, feel your body, listen to the buzz in your ears, and allow yourself to be present without doing nothing. Take advantage of this opportunity to understand more.

Tune in to your breath's natural rhythm, whatever it may be at the present moment. You can breathe without manipulation. Be conscious of your body position in your practice. Keep your mind engaged by scanning your body. Regular practice will make the process enjoyable for you.

Slow down your mind's rapid movements and reach the state of self-awareness where miracles happen. Instead of asking the universe for things, believe that you deserve everything you desire.

It's your job to have unwavering faith that everything you aspire to is already yours. You will feel a sense of accomplishment investing in yourself. Reminding yourself you are a moving, breathing tabernacle dancing to the rhythm of your heart can be an empowering booster.

LOOKING FOR A PLAN TO TAKE ACTION

When I think back to recovering from knee surgery, I remember feeling an urgent need for a plan. The thought of my father being bedridden and unable to move for three years haunted me. I recall my eleven-year-old self gazing at my god lying in bed, questioning what had happened to him. I made a promise then that his experience was not mine and would never be.

Even on his deathbed, he was an extraordinary father. I couldn't sense any pity or sympathy coming from him. He was always in a good mood, and laughing and falling frequently on his way to the outdoor toilet. Each time, he would lie on his back and laugh. He was an immense god who needed support while walking, so my sister and I walked with him, holding him under his armpits while our two younger brothers assisted us. The comedy play involved going back and forth between the house and the outdoor toilet. His example helped me to resist the urge to seek sympathy when I was feeling down. I took inspiration from my god's tendency to rise after a fall and asked myself, why couldn't I do the same?

A speaker once emphasized to his audience the importance of paying attention and investing in assimilating information. His suggestion to the group was to achieve mastery of their subject and to teach it to others. The speaker believes that by paying it forward, students can imagine a broader perspective of life and its interconnectedness.

A Story About the Man and His Lantern

Diogenes the Cynic (404 BC), Greek philosopher and citizen of Athens, walked among the people with a lit lantern in broad daylight, according to the belief. When asked why he was walking around in the middle of the day with a lantern, he responded, "I am looking for an honest man."

When taken as a metaphor, the honest man or woman represents the being within. Just like my father, the wind of death could never snuff out his light because he reflects light, as we all do. The human temple body is the lamp that, when filled with visions (oil) from the source, will naturally radiate from within. As you engage in the refilling of your lantern with your daily practice, your efforts will shine in your life with ease. It is you who creates your experiences.

IMPLEMENT THE PRINCIPLES

Perform the exercises outlined in this book. You stand to gain everything and lose nothing in your forward movements. What makes you shine? Your answer has the potential to open doors for sharing your story. Own your creative power.

Our conversation focuses on the theme of taking control of your life. We discussed ways to relax, achieve inner balance, and synchronize our thoughts with our bodies. We learned from the chapter about forgiveness that two states cannot occupy the same space.

During your practice, you may discover how the mind can easily stray from your aim and become preoccupied with self-doubt and criticism. It's easier to talk about managing the mind than doing it. I suggest you consider viewing this practice of seeing from behind your eyes as a meditation in your daily routine. Wherever you are, whatever you are doing, be there now. Allow anything that hinders your potential to drift away like clouds.

You might be thinking, *How can I implement the principles shared in this book?* Well, during the second editing of this book, I started taking swimming lessons. I stepped up my game and challenged myself to overcome the fear of drowning.

For decades, I lived with the shame of having to be rescued in a swimming pool during my teens. This dreaded feeling makes me believe I'm too old to learn to swim. It wasn't until I questioned my argument about age and asked myself, "What am I saying?" that I realized the truth. My age is only a measurement of a mechanical device, a time concept in the form of a human clock. So, I remind myself that my daily work is a meditation. With a profound change in perspective, I signed up for the wonderful challenge.

It's a liberating feeling knowing that you are the sum of all your experiences. You are an ordinary being, experiencing life as it is. All your visions and aspirations are a part of the one conscious being, which is you.

CONCLUSION

I consulted a business coach about the importance of discomfort in the learning process. He responded, "The real 'you' will keep knocking you around until you surrender to the natural flow."

Emotions seek expressions because they are energy in motion. Your ongoing projection of energy influences the reality you perceive.

Individuals don't use drugs intending to end their lives. They are looking for a temporary solution to their uneasiness.

At a lecture I was giving, a woman asked, "Why is it so challenging to transition from feeling down to feeling good?"

I took a brief pause before responding to ensure I comprehended her question. My answer was that the mind influences the body. Next, I shared an example of a drunk person struggling to stay upright. Excessive alcohol intoxicates the mind, leading to a drunken body.

If feeling good is a challenge, let's start by altering the body's physiology. We can achieve a shift in your mind by walking in the park, holding your head high, relaxing your shoulders, and grounding your weight down to your feet. In the latter part of the week, a couple of audience members practiced moves that were comparable to exercises mentioned in part 1 of this book.

After becoming acquainted with these exercises and being able to perform them through memory, a multitude of choices will be at your disposal whenever necessary. Zero in on finding your center. Integrate alignment, relaxation, and balance into your body matrix while visualizing yourself within the center of an imaginary balloon.

Use every opportunity to envision yourself rooted in the fundamental principles outlined in this book. Incorporate them as guiding points in your life. You'll be amazed at the level of connection you feel within your body. Incorporate them into your self-talk throughout your day. Recite them like a mantra. Don't forget, you can shape your own subjective reality. Craft a life that is tailored to your needs. A life that is both beautiful and truthful.

Shape your life to match your vision. Find peace in knowing that all the dualities you see in life have a single source. You are the one taking part in the game of life. Embracing unity and seeking fresh options is crucial for embracing change. Gather momentum like lava from a volcano, heading toward fertile ground.

Two principles reflect your potential energy as an artist dreamer: The infinite dance of yin and yang, forever spiraling behind your eyes.

What is your desired outcome?

Make a promise to yourself to create something beautiful. Stay vigilant for any negative or self-doubting thoughts that arise. Allow them to flow upon arrival. Internal expansion and vitality result from a solid and focused foundation.

Success Can Be Obtained by Taking Small Steps

Starting with an unstable foundation can lead to a lifetime of problem-solving. Here is a demoralizing thought that can ruin your progress. You wish you could afford a personal trainer because getting in shape seems like an enormous task that requires both time and money. Well, take the stairs instead of the escalator. Small actions interrupt the mind's excuses for not starting.

Finding Your Joy

Unmotivated thoughts are never your fault, but it's your responsibility to make a change. Laugh at those silly thoughts and scream like a crazy child on a roller coaster. Daily practice can transform your journey into a meditative experience. Your perseverance is the strength that helps you observe and achieve success. As you progress in your work, it will surprise you how expansive your goals become. It's like attempting to touch a dragonfly. It dances in stillness, allowing you to approach before dashing away. Be smart with your practice. Block out twenty minutes for yourself on each day. Elevate your conscious awareness by transforming your hands into wings.

To conclude our conversation, I'll leave you with a quote from Neville Goddard: "All changes take place in consciousness. The future, although prepared in every detail in advance, has several outcomes."[15]

Abundant Blessings, wherever your journey takes you.

—Evan Worldwind

---

[15] Neville Goddard. Resurrection Out of This world, Thinking fourth-Dimensionally, page 110. DeVorse Publications.

ABOUT THE AUTHOR

Evan Worldwind's journey into the transformational arts has spanned over more than twenty years. He is a certified Neuro-Linguistic Re-Visioning coach and a practitioner of the Yang Family Style of Tai Chi Chuan.

His great love for storytelling combined with his impressive skills in tai chi and the didgeridoo—the traditional wind instrument of the Aboriginal People of Australia—have given him a voice on stage.

He has captivated audiences across New York, from the esteemed Chapel of Sacred Mirrors committee to attendees of Brushwood's Sirius Rising and the Woodstock Fruit Festival. He currently lives between New York City in the United States and Barcelona, Spain.

For more information about Evan Worldwind and his extended work, please visit www.artistdreamfamily.com

APPRECIATION

If you're willing, He would greatly appreciate a brief and honest loudspeaker review at the given link: https://www.artistdreamfamily.com/contacts.

ABOUT THE BOOK COVER ILLUSTRATION

The illustration on the cover of this book presents the idea of perceiving reality from within. The magnetic waves spiraling from the circle's circumference represent desires and goals.

At the center of the image, there is a circle presenting a single eye, revealing a hidden world.

"If therefore thine eyes be single, thy whole body shall be full of light."

Within you, the reader, lies the beautiful, powerful, and unified light.

BIBLIOGRAPHY

Bontrager, Will. "Number 36 Meaning." *Affinity Numerology*. Will Bontrager Software LLC. Accessed September 19, 2023. https://affinitynumerology.com/number-meanings/number-36-meaning.php.

Bontrager, Will. "Number 9 Meaning." *Affinity Numerology*. Will Bontrager Software LLC. Accessed September 19, 2023. https://affinitynumerology.com/number-meanings/number-9-meaning.php.

Camacho, Natalie Arroyo and Rebecca Norris. "The Angel Number 4 is Basically Your Ancestors Giving You a Support Hug." *Well and Good*. Last modified August 25, 2023. https://www.wellandgood.com/angel-number-4.

Goddard, Neville. "There is No Fiction." *Real Neville*. Accessed September 19, 2023. https://realneville.com/txt/there_is_no_fiction.htm.

Morgan, Marlo. *Mutant Message Down Under*. New York: Harper Collins. 2009.

Scoop, Sarah. "The Meaning and Symbolism of the Angel Number 13 in Numerology." *Sarah Scoop*. Accessed September 19, 2023. https://sarahscoop.com/the-meaning-and-symbolism-of-the-angel-number-13-in-numerology.

www.ingramcontent.com/pod-product-compliance
Lightning Source LLC
Chambersburg PA
CBHW071700170426
43195CB00039B/2370